THE TIMES TOP 100 GRADUATE EMPLOYERS

The definitive guide to the leading employers recruiting graduates during 2022-2023.

HIGH FLIERS

HIGH FLIERS PUBLICATIONS LTD
IN ASSOCIATION WITH THE TIMES

Published by High Fliers Publications Limited
The Gridiron Building, 1 Pancras Square, London, N1C 4AG
Telephone: 020 7428 9100   *Web:* www.Top100GraduateEmployers.com

Editor Martin Birchall
Publisher Gill Thomas
Production Manager Darcy Mackay
Portrait Photography www.cityspacecreative.co.uk

The Times Top 100 Graduate Employers is based on research
results from *The UK Graduate Careers Survey 2022*,
produced by High Fliers Research Ltd.

The greatest care has been taken in compiling this book.
However, no responsibility can be accepted by the publishers
or compilers for the accuracy of the information presented.

Where opinion is expressed it is that of the author or advertiser
and does not necessarily coincide with the editorial views of
High Fliers Publications Limited or *The Times* newspaper.

Printed and bound in Italy by L.E.G.O. S.p.A.

A CIP catalogue record for this book
is available from the British Library.
ISBN 978-1-9160401-3-7

Contents

Foreword

By **Martin Birchall**
Editor, *The Times Top 100 Graduate Employers*

Welcome to the 2022-2023 edition of *The Times Top 100 Graduate Employers*, your annual guide to the UK's most prestigious and sought-after graduate employers.

This year has seen the UK thrust into unprecedented political and economic turmoil. After more than fifty members of Parliament resigned from Boris Johnson's government in less than 48 hours – including five cabinet ministers – the country now has its fourth prime minister in just six years.

And the latest dire warnings from the Bank of England are that inflation will reach 13 per cent by the end of the year, the UK will be in recession throughout 2023, and the country is facing its worst cost-of-living crisis since the 1970s – brought on by the aftermath of the Coronavirus pandemic, Russia's invasion of Ukraine, and global energy shortages.

This surge in inflation has already had an impact on university graduates – the interest rate charged on student loans is now a daunting 6.3 per cent, and could have jumped to double this, without a hastily-introduced government cap on the rate.

The higher interest rate coincides with next year's reduction in the repayment threshold, so that graduates earning salaries of £25,000 or more will have to make student loan repayments. The repayment period has been extended too – from thirty to forty years – meaning most graduates will be repaying their student debts well into their 60s.

None of this makes encouraging reading if you are one of the 400,000 final year students due to be leaving university in 2023, especially as so much of student life over the past two years has been decimated by the pandemic, with lectures and exams switched online, little or no face-to-face teaching, reduced access to campuses, and social 'bubbles' for students living in university accommodation.

But the encouraging news is that the graduate job market has recovered very strongly from the effects of the pandemic. Graduate vacancies at the UK's leading employers reached at all-time high in 2022, up by 11 per cent compared with pre-pandemic recruitment.

And the outlook for 2023 remains upbeat, with employers in almost all of the key industries and business sectors expecting to expand their graduate recruitment in the next 12 months.

During the pandemic, almost every aspect of recruitment was moved online. The country's best-known employers promoted their graduate vacancies through virtual careers fairs and online presentations, rather than their usual programme of on-campus promotions, and used fully-online selection and assessment processes for applicants.

❝ Many of the UK's best-known employers will be returning to campus for the 2022-2023 graduate recruitment round.❞

Although some students found the new era of online recruitment more convenient, two-fifths of final year students from the 'Class of 2022' said it had been harder to find out which employers were offering graduate vacancies and a third complained that it had been more difficult to have one-to-one conversations with recruiters or recent graduates.

Happily, many of the UK's best-known employers will be returning to campus for the 2022-2023 graduate recruitment round, to take part in university careers fairs and host their own recruitment presentations and skills events. But a significant number of employers are intending to continue with their online-led graduate recruitment processes for the year ahead.

An overwhelming 87 per cent of new graduates who left university in the summer of 2022 believed that now all of the pandemic restrictions have been lifted, graduate employers should use to a mix of in-person, on-campus events and online promotions, rather than a fully online approach for their graduate recruitment.

The editorial features in this edition of The Times Top 100 Graduate Employers examine how the graduate job market has recovered from the impact of pandemic, the employment outlook for next year's university-leavers, as well as analysing the new Top 100 rankings and providing advice, guidance and practical tips on successful graduate job hunting and preparing for the post-pandemic working world.

Since the first edition was published in 1999, more than a million copies of The Times Top 100 Graduate Employers have now been produced, helping students and graduates at universities across the UK to research their career options and find their first graduate job.

And over the past two years, over 100,000 job hunters have read the popular new digital edition of the Top 100 that was introduced at the beginning of the pandemic.

More than two decades after its launch, The Times Top 100 Graduate Employers continues to provide an unrivalled, independent assessment of the UK's most highly-rated graduate employers.

It won't necessarily identify which organisation you should join after graduation – only you can decide that. But it is an invaluable reference, especially in uncertain times, if you want to discover what the country's leading employers are offering for new graduates in 2023.

THE TIMES TOP 100 GRADUATE EMPLOYERS — Finding out about the Top 100 Graduate Employers

PRINT & DIGITAL EDITION

Each employer featured in this edition of the Top 100 has their own **Employer Entry**, providing details of graduate vacancies for 2023, minimum academic requirements, starting salaries, for new graduates, plus this year's application deadlines.

WEBSITE

Register now with the official Top 100 website for full access to the very latest information about the UK's most sought-after graduate employers.

This includes details of employers' internships & work experience programmes, local university promotions and application deadlines.

And get ready for your applications, online interviews and assessment centres with up-to-the-minute business news about each of the organisations featured in this year's Top 100.

www.Top100GraduateEmployers.com

BY EMAIL

Once you've registered with the Top 100 website, you'll receive **weekly email bulletins** with news of the employers you're interested in, details of their latest graduate vacancies, and their forthcoming application deadlines.

pwc

Join our community of solvers

The New Equation is our global strategy to address the breadth and complexity of challenges facing our clients and communities. We work together to build trust and deliver sustained outcomes by combining human ingenuity with the right technology for real results.

Be a part of The New Equation

To find out more, visit: **pwc.co.uk/careers**

Civil Service
Fast Stream

" We need talented graduates with degrees in the areas of science, technology, engineering and maths to join the civil service. With the spotlight on science in recent years, this is a very exciting time to join the Fast Stream and use your expertise to help us keep science and engineering at the heart of big government decisions. "

Sir Patrick Vallance

www.faststream.gov.uk

Meet Rian

He was studying for a master's degree in Physics at the University of Liverpool when he first learned about the Civil Service Fast Stream programme. He wanted to join a team where he could make a real impact on the lives of others, so when he was first posted to the Established Renewables Policy Team as a Scientific Adviser, it felt like the perfect match – and he didn't even have to leave Liverpool to make it happen.

He provides scientific support that helps inform energy policy – from researching the biggest challenges the UK currently faces in this sector, to exploring exciting new solar technology developments.

Rian's STEM degree made him the perfect candidate for his choice of scheme, but you don't have to have a STEM background to find a role that suits you. Whether it's in finance, human resources, politics, engineering, data, technology, or economics, our Fast Stream programme opens an almost unlimited number of career paths for you to choose from.

FROM *studying physics* **TO** working on renewable energy policy

THE TIMES

TOP 100 GRADUATE EMPLOYERS 2014-2015

THE TIMES

TOP 100 GRADUATE EMPLOYERS 2015-2016

THE TIMES

TOP 100 GRADUATE EMPLOYERS 2016-2017

THE TIMES

TOP 100 GRADUATE EMPLOYERS 2017-2018

THE TIMES

TOP 100 GRADUATE EMPLOYERS 2018-2019

THE TIMES

TOP 100 GRADUATE EMPLOYERS 2019-2020

THE TIMES

TOP 100 GRADUATE EMPLOYERS 2020-2021

THE TIMES

TOP 100 GRADUATE EMPLOYERS 2021-2022

THE TIMES

TOP 100 GRADUATE EMPLOYERS 2022-2023

Researching The Times Top 100 Graduate Employers

By **Gill Thomas**
Publisher, High Fliers Publications

When the first edition of *The Times Top 100 Graduate Employers* was published in 1999, there were an estimated five thousand employers, large and small, recruiting graduates from the UK's leading universities.

The number of employers recruiting graduates has risen steadily over the past two decades and there are now currently more than 200,000 graduate-level vacancies available for university-leavers annually.

For students researching their career options, finding the 'right' graduate employer can often be a daunting prospect. What basis can you use to evaluate such a large number of different organisations and the opportunities they offer for new graduates after university?

The Times Top 100 Graduate Employers is compiled annually by the independent market research company, High Fliers Research, through interviews with final year students at the country's leading universities.

This latest edition is based on research with 12,432 students who were due to graduate from universities across the UK in the summer of 2022. The research examined students' experiences during their search for a first graduate job and asked them about their attitudes to employers.

Final year students from the 'Class of 2022' who took part in the study were selected at random to represent the full cross-section of finalists at their universities, not just those who had already secured graduate employment.

The question used to produce the *Top 100* rankings was "Which employer do you think offers the best opportunities for graduates?". The question was deliberately open-ended and students were not shown a list of employers to choose from or prompted during the interview.

The wide selection of answers given during the research shows that final year students used very different criteria to decide which employer offered the best opportunities for graduates. Some evaluated employers based on the quality of the recruitment promotions they'd seen whilst at university – either online or in-person – or their recent experiences during the application and graduate selection process.

Other final year students used the 'graduate employment proposition' as their main guide – the quality of training and development an employer offers, the starting salary and remuneration package available, and the practical aspects of a first graduate job, such as its location or the likely working hours.

Across the full survey sample, final year students named more than 900 different organisations – noticeably fewer than previous years – but

> **❝** *In an impressive achievement, the Civil Service is ranked the UK's number one graduate employer for the fourth consecutive year.* **❞**

THE TIMES TOP 100 GRADUATE EMPLOYERS

The Times Top 100 Graduate Employers 2022

	2021				2021	
1	1	CIVIL SERVICE		51	49	BDO
2	3	NHS		52	60	WHITE & CASE
3	2	PWC		53	59	UBS
4	4	DELOITTE		54	74	BAIN & COMPANY
5	7	GOOGLE		55	41	TESCO
6	6	EY		56	61	HERBERT SMITH FREEHILLS
7	8	BBC		57	57	DEUTSCHE BANK
8	10	KPMG		58	75	MCDONALD'S
9	5	ALDI		59	79	MI5
10	14	AMAZON		60	83	CMS
11	17	GOLDMAN SACHS		61	86	BANK OF AMERICA
12	12	J.P. MORGAN		62	91	BANK OF ENGLAND
13	11	GSK (now GSK & Haleon)		63	93	JAGUAR LAND ROVER
14	9	TEACH FIRST		64	54	ROYAL NAVY
15	15	BARCLAYS		65	78	IRWIN MITCHELL
16	13	HSBC		66	NEW	BMW GROUP
17	25	CLIFFORD CHANCE		67	51	UNLOCKED GRADUATES
18	22	MCKINSEY & COMPANY		68	66	SAVILLS
19	21	L'ORÉAL		69	76	PFIZER
20	16	UNILEVER		70	NEW	JANE STREET
21	19	LINKLATERS		71	64	DYSON
22	20	ASTRAZENECA		72	NEW	SANTANDER
23	26	ROLLS-ROYCE		73	50	LOCAL GOVERNMENT
24	24	ARUP		74	52	BAKER MCKENZIE
25	29	BAE SYSTEMS		75	69	AIRBUS
26	30	ACCENTURE		76	90	SHELL
27	33	SKY		77	NEW	ARCADIS
28	40	LLOYDS BANKING GROUP		78	NEW	SPECSAVERS
29	45	MORGAN STANLEY		79	77	GCHQ
30	38	BOSTON CONSULTING GROUP		80	82	MARS
31	23	BRITISH ARMY		81	NEW	TIKTOK
32	44	NEWTON		82	NEW	AON
33	27	ALLEN & OVERY		83	NEW	CREDIT SUISSE
34	36	LIDL		84	NEW	HUGH JAMES
35	37	NATWEST GROUP		85	NEW	PA CONSULTING
36	46	SLAUGHTER AND MAY		86	39	THINK AHEAD
37	62	APPLE		87	72	THG
38	28	POLICE NOW		88	80	FRESHFIELDS
39	18	PROCTER & GAMBLE		89	87	KUBRICK
40	42	BP		90	98	LATHAM & WATKINS
41	56	CITI		91	NEW	CLYDE & CO
42	63	BLOOMBERG		92	NEW	EVERSHEDS SUTHERLAND
43	32	FRONTLINE		93	NEW	REED SMITH
44	47	MICROSOFT		94	70	TPP
45	34	IBM		95	84	HOGAN LOVELLS
46	31	PENGUIN RANDOM HOUSE		96	88	GRANT THORNTON
47	35	BT		97	92	PEPSICO
48	65	ATKINS		98	94	MOTT MACDONALD
49	68	BLACKROCK		99	95	ENTERPRISE
50	71	VODAFONE		100	NEW	AMERICAN EXPRESS

Source **High Fliers Research** 12,432 final year students leaving UK universities in the summer of 2022 were asked the open-ended question "Which employer do you think offers the best opportunities for graduates?" during interviews for *The UK Graduate Careers Survey 2022* these ranged from well-known national and international organisations, to small and medium-sized regional and local employers. The responses were analysed and the one hundred organisations that were named most often make up *The Times Top 100 Graduate Employers* for 2022.

In an impressive achievement, the Civil Service is ranked the UK's number one graduate employer for the fourth consecutive year. Best known for its prestigious Fast Stream programme, 5.6 per cent of final year students from the 'Class of 2022' voted for the Civil Service, which was more than two hundred votes ahead of the next most popular employer in this year's league table.

After two years at the forefront of the UK's response to the Coronavirus pandemic, the NHS moves up to second place, its best-ever ranking in the *Top 100*. As a result, the 'Big Four' accounting & professional services firm PwC, which held the number one position for fifteen years until 2018, slips back to third place.

Rival professional services firms Deloitte and EY are unchanged in fourth and sixth places respectively, but Google moves back up two places and the BBC is up to seventh place, its best ranking for a decade. Retailer Aldi slips down to ninth place, taking it out of the top five for the first time since 2013. After appearing as a new entry in 2015 in 81st place and rising up the rankings in each of the following six years, Amazon has now reached the top ten, having climbed another four places this year.

Investment bank Goldman Sachs is up six places to 11th place, overtaking J.P. Morgan, HSBC and Barclays. GSK – the chemical & pharmaceuticals company which recently demerged its consumer healthcare business into a new company, Haleon – slips two places to 13th place. Law firm Clifford Chance climbs into the top twenty for the first time and both McKinsey & Company and L'Oréal have also achieved their highest-ever rankings.

Within the new *Top 100*, the year's highest climbers are led by Jaguar Land Rover, which has rebounded an impressive thirty places to 63rd place, following an even bigger fall in last year's rankings. The Bank of England is up twenty-nine places to 62nd place, its best ranking yet. Bank of America and Apple have both jumped twenty-five places and CMS, Vodafone, Bloomberg, MI5 - The Security Service, Bain & Company, and Blackrock have each climbed at least twenty places in this year's *Top 100*.

The biggest fallers of the year include Think Ahead, the mental health graduate programme, which has dropped forty-seven places from 39th in 2020 to 86th place this year. Consumer goods company Procter & Gamble is down twenty-one places to 39th place, its lowest-ever ranking. Technology company TPP, Local Government and law firm Baker McKenzie have each fallen at least twenty places in the new rankings.

There are fourteen new entries or re-entries in this year's *Top 100*, the second-largest changeover of ranked employers in the twenty-four year history of *The Times Top 100 Graduate Employers*.

The highest new entry is for the BMW Group, which returns in 66th place, its best-ever ranking. It is joined by the global traders Jane Street, engineering & design company Arcadis, Specsavers, social media favourite TikTok, professional services company Aon, and law firms Hugh James, Clyde & Co and Reed Smith – all of which are ranked for the first time.

PA Consulting has returned to the *Top 100* for the first time since 2005, along with Santander, Credit Suisse, law firm Eversheds Sutherland, and American Express, which are re-entries in the new *Top 100*. There are now a total of sixteen law firms in this year's *Top 100*, a record number of employers from a single industry or business sector within the rankings.

The bumper crop of new entries, both this year and last year, means that a fifth of the employers that appeared in *The Times Top 100 Graduate Employers* in 2020 – the final rankings before the onset of the Coronavirus pandemic – are now no longer ranked. Among the fourteen employers leaving the *Top 100* in 2022 are CharityWorks, the graduate charity programme that was ranked in 43rd place last year, and the charitable foundation Wellcome, which has featured in the *Top 100* for the past seven years.

Other employers that have left this year's league table include Siemens, Channel Four, engineering firm AECOM, and law firm DLA Piper and eight employers that were new or re-entries in the 2021 rankings – ITV, Nestlé, Red Bull, ARM, The Walt Disney Company, RSM, Mazars and Diageo.

Since the original edition of *The Times Top 100 Graduate Employers* was published more than two decades ago, just three organisations have made it to number one in the rankings. Andersen Consulting (now Accenture) held on to the top spot for the first four years, and its success heralded a

Be part of
the next trend.

ACCOUNTANCY WILL
GET YOU THERE.

huge surge in popularity for careers in consulting. At its peak in 2001, almost one in six graduates applied for jobs in the sector.

In the year before the firm changed its name from Andersen Consulting to Accenture, it astutely introduced a new graduate package that included a £28,500 starting salary (a sky-high figure for graduates in 2000) and a much-talked-about £10,000 bonus, helping to assure the firm's popularity, irrespective of its corporate branding.

In 2003, after two dismal years in graduate recruitment when vacancies for university-leavers dropped by more than a fifth following the terrorist attacks of 11th September 2001, the Civil Service was named the UK's leading graduate employer.

Just twelve months later it was displaced by PricewaterhouseCoopers, the accounting and professional services firm formed from the merger of Price Waterhouse and Coopers & Lybrand in 1998. At the time, the firm was the largest private sector recruiter of graduates, with an intake in 2004 of more than a thousand trainees.

Now known simply as PwC, the firm remained at number one for an impressive fifteen years, increasing its share of the student vote from 5 per cent in 2004 to more than 10 per cent in 2007, and fighting off the stiffest of competition from rivals Deloitte in 2008, when just seven votes separated the two employers.

PwC's reign as the UK's leading graduate employer represented a real renaissance for the entire accounting & professional services sector. Twenty years ago, a career in accountancy was regarded as a safe, traditional employment choice, whereas today's profession is viewed in a very different light. The training required to become a chartered accountant is now seen as a prized business qualification, and the sector's leading firms are regularly described as 'dynamic' and 'international' by undergraduates looking for their first job after university.

A total of 232 different organisations have now appeared within *The Times Top 100 Graduate Employers* since its inception, and thirty-six of these have made it into the rankings every year since 1999.

The most consistent performers have been PwC, KPMG and the Civil Service, each of which have never been lower than 10th place in the league table. The NHS has also had a formidable record,

THE TIMES TOP 100 GRADUATE EMPLOYERS — Number Ones, Movers & Shakers in the Top 100

	NUMBER ONES		HIGHEST CLIMBING EMPLOYERS		HIGHEST NEW ENTRIES
1999	ANDERSEN CONSULTING	1999	SCHLUMBERGER (UP 13 PLACES)	1999	PFIZER (31st)
2000	ANDERSEN CONSULTING	2000	CAPITAL ONE (UP 32 PLACES)	2000	MORGAN STANLEY (34th)
2001	ACCENTURE	2001	EUROPEAN COMMISSION (UP 36 PLACES)	2001	MARCONI (36th)
2002	ACCENTURE	2002	WPP (UP 36 PLACES)	2002	GUINNESS UDV (44th)
2003	CIVIL SERVICE	2003	ROLLS-ROYCE (UP 37 PLACES)	2003	ASDA (40th)
2004	PRICEWATERHOUSECOOPERS	2004	J.P. MORGAN (UP 29 PLACES)	2004	BAKER & MCKENZIE (61st)
2005	PRICEWATERHOUSECOOPERS	2005	TEACH FIRST (UP 22 PLACES)	2005	PENGUIN (70th)
2006	PRICEWATERHOUSECOOPERS	2006	GOOGLE (UP 32 PLACES)	2006	FUJITSU (81st)
2007	PRICEWATERHOUSECOOPERS	2007	PFIZER (UP 30 PLACES)	2007	BDO STOY HAYWARD (74th)
2008	PRICEWATERHOUSECOOPERS	2008	CO-OPERATIVE GROUP (UP 39 PLACES)	2008	SKY (76th)
2009	PRICEWATERHOUSECOOPERS	2009	CADBURY (UP 48 PLACES)	2009	BDO STOY HAYWARD (68th)
2010	PRICEWATERHOUSECOOPERS	2010	ASDA (UP 41 PLACES)	2010	SAATCHI & SAATCHI (49th)
2011	PWC	2011	CENTRICA (UP 41 PLACES)	2011	APPLE (53rd)
2012	PWC	2012	NESTLÉ (UP 44 PLACES)	2012	EUROPEAN COMMISSION (56th)
2013	PWC	2013	DFID (UP 40 PLACES)	2013	SIEMENS (70th)
2014	PWC	2014	TRANSPORT FOR LONDON (UP 36 PLACES)	2014	FRONTLINE (76th)
2015	PWC	2015	DIAGEO, NEWTON (UP 43 PLACES)	2015	DANONE (66th)
2016	PWC	2016	BANK OF ENGLAND (UP 34 PLACES)	2016	SANTANDER (63rd)
2017	PWC	2017	CANCER RESEARCH UK (UP 38 PLACES)	2017	DYSON (52nd)
2018	PWC	2018	MCDONALD'S (UP 30 PLACES)	2018	ASOS (52nd)
2019	CIVIL SERVICE	2019	POLICE NOW (UP 43 PLACES)	2019	UNLOCKED (49th)
2020	CIVIL SERVICE	2020	DLA PIPER / WHITE & CASE (UP 32 PLACES)	2020	CHANNEL FOUR (77th)
2021	CIVIL SERVICE	2021	CHARITYWORKS (UP 45 PLACES)	2021	BDO (49th)
2022	CIVIL SERVICE	2022	JAGUAR LAND ROVER (UP 30 PLACES)	2022	BMW GROUP (66th)

Source High Fliers Research

appearing in every top ten since 2003, while the BBC, Goldman Sachs and EY (formerly Ernst & Young) have all remained within the top twenty throughout the last decade.

Google is the highest-climbing employer within the *Top 100*, having risen over eighty places during the last decade, to reach the top three for the first time in 2015. But car manufacturer Jaguar Land Rover holds the record for the fastest-moving employer, after jumping more than seventy places in just five years, between 2009 and 2014.

Other employers haven't been so successful. British Airways ranked in 6th place in 1999 but dropped out of the *Top 100* a decade later, and Ford, which was once rated as high as 14th, disappeared out of the list in 2006 after cancelling its graduate recruitment programme two years previously. More recent high-ranking casualties include the John Lewis Partnership which – having been 9th in 2003 – tumbled out of the *Top 100* in 2020 and Marks & Spencer which was in 7th place in the inaugural *Top 100* in 1999, dropped out of last year's rankings altogether.

More than thirty graduate employers – including Nokia, Maersk, the Home Office, Cable & Wireless, United Biscuits, Nationwide, Capgemini and the Met Office – have the dubious record of having only been ranked in the *Top 100* once during the last twenty years. And Marconi had the unusual distinction of being one of the highest-ever new entries, in 36th place in 2001, only to vanish from the list entirely the following year.

One of the most spectacular ascendancies in the *Top 100* has been the rise of Aldi, which joined the list in 65th place in 2002, rose to 3rd place in 2009 – helped in part by its memorable remuneration

THE TIMES TOP 100 GRADUATE EMPLOYERS — Winners & Losers in the Top 100

MOST CONSISTENT EMPLOYERS	HIGHEST RANKING	LOWEST RANKING
PWC	1st (2004-2018)	3rd (1999-2001, 2003, 2022)
CIVIL SERVICE	1st (2003, 2019-2022)	8th (2011)
KPMG	3rd (2006-2008, 2011-2012)	10th (2021)
BBC	5th (2005-2007)	14th (1999)
GSK	10th (2017-2018)	22nd (2002-2003)
EY (FORMERLY ERNST & YOUNG)	6th (2021)	20th (2001)
GOLDMAN SACHS	5th (2001)	25th (1999)
BARCLAYS	12th (2013)	35th (2006)
HSBC	6th (2003)	29th (1999)
NHS	2nd (2022)	27th (1999, 2002)

EMPLOYERS CLIMBING HIGHEST	NEW ENTRY RANKING	HIGHEST RANKING
GOOGLE	85th (2005)	3rd (2015)
LIDL	89th (2009)	13th (2017)
NEWTON	94th (2013)	19th (2019)
AMAZON	81st (2015)	10th (2022)
JAGUAR LAND ROVER	87th (2009)	16th (2014)
ALDI	65th (2002)	2nd (2015-2016)
MI5 – THE SECURITY SERVICE	96th (2007)	33rd (2010)
POLICE NOW	90th (2018)	28th (2021)
TEACH FIRST	63rd (2003)	2nd (2014)
APPLE	87th (2009)	27th (2012)

EMPLOYERS FALLING FURTHEST	HIGHEST RANKING	LOWEST RANKING
BRITISH AIRWAYS	6th (1999)	Not ranked (2010, 2011, 2017, FROM 2019)
MARKS & SPENCER	7th (1999)	Not ranked (FROM 2021)
JOHN LEWIS PARTNERSHIP	9th (2013)	Not ranked (FROM 2020)
BOOTS	10th (1999)	Not ranked (FROM 2021)
FORD	11th (1999)	Not ranked (FROM 2006)
UBS	17th (2002)	Not ranked (2018)
SAINSBURY'S	18th (2003)	Not ranked (FROM 2016)
EXXONMOBIL	19th (1999)	Not ranked (FROM 2021)
SHELL	11th (2006)	90th (2021)
THOMSON REUTERS	22nd (2001)	Not ranked (2009-2012, FROM 2014)

Source High Fliers Research

ICAS

Zahrah Mahmood
Summit-seeking
Chartered Accountant

CALLING ALL TRAILBLAZERS

LAUNCH YOUR CAREER AS A CHARTERED ACCOUNTANT

icas.com/becomeaca

package for new recruits (currently £44,000 plus a fully-expensed VW electric car) – and was ranked in 2nd place in both 2015 and 2016.

Teach First, the first of five inspirational schemes that are transforming society by bringing top graduates into public service, appeared as a new entry in 63rd place in 2003, before climbing the rankings every year for a decade and reaching 2nd place in the *Top 100* in 2014. Over the last three years another of these programmes, Police Now, has jumped more than sixty places from 90th in 2018 to 28th place in the 2021 rankings.

This year's edition of *The Times Top 100 Graduate Employers* has produced a number of dramatic changes within the rankings, and the results provide a unique insight into how graduates from the 'Class of 2022' rated the country's leading employers.

THE TIMES TOP 100 GRADUATE EMPLOYERS
The UK's Number 1 Graduate Employer 2022

"We are delighted that the Civil Service is number one in *The Times Top 100 Graduate Employers* for the fourth year running.

It's a real testament to the work we've done to improve the quality of training and the quality of the experience that the Civil Service Fast Stream offers new graduates – and it's a privilege to have that recognised again in this year's rankings.

Over the past two years, as a result of the pandemic, we've seen a real shift in thinking. More and more graduates look to contribute to the wider good and become public servants, whether that be in shaping policy at national or local level or working on longer-term global issues like climate change.

The Fast Stream has attracted more than 40,000 applications this year and we've seen a steady increase in interest for our speciality schemes like science and engineering, and the digital and data scheme.

We take being the nation's number one graduate employer very seriously and that means we're looking to continually improve and evolve what the Fast Stream offers.

As part of wider Civil Service reforms, we have a programme underway to transform the Fast Stream. How it is marketed, its training content and how it delivers the core skills, knowledge and experience that the Civil Service and government need to work effectively in the future.

Because of this transformation, we're not intending to recruit for the Fast Stream in 2023, but there will continue to be other routes into the Civil Service for graduates, including direct entry routes.

Sonia Pawson, Head of the Civil Service Fast Stream

And the Civil Service Fast Stream will be expanding its internships for summer 2023, with opportunities open to all undergraduates and recent graduates, irrespective of their subject background or location.

These are a great way to boost employability skills, gain transferable knowledge and develop networks, and would be excellent preparation for students and graduates intending to apply for the Fast Stream when we re-open for applications.

We are continuing to work closely with universities across the UK and will be taking part in campus events and promotions in the coming months. "

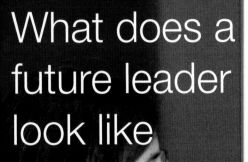

What does a
future leader
look like

today?

We're building a bank that's fit for
the future, now. It's why we welcome
applications to our Global Internships
and Graduate Programmes from
students and graduates with any
degree, from any background.

hsbc.com/earlycareers

 HSBC

Shaping lives has never been so rewarding.

Teaching translates your passion for your subject into a career that's **life-changing** – not just for you, but for those you teach.

It's endlessly rewarding – in more ways than one. You'll receive a generous holiday allowance of up to 13 weeks; allowing you more time to do what you love, and to bring those hobbies into the classroom. You'll also be entitled to a great pension package; progressing in a career that's both **exciting** and **secure**.

Most importantly, you'll get the chance to shape lives every day, making a difference to those it matters to most. With a career package that's just as rewarding as the lessons you teach, it's presenting graduates, just like you with a decision that's never been easier.

Ready?

Search: **Get Into Teaching**

Department
for Education

Manny Awoyelu
Assistant Headteache

Eastbury Community
School

"To me, teaching is about empowering young people, changing lives, making a difference and equipping young people with the tools to be better individuals for the future. It's incredibly fulfilling.

I wake up every day proud and honoured to be in the role. I come into school and there's faces, you know, young children smiling at you because you are the first person they're seeing today who has said good morning to them. It's those little interactions that I think make the difference.

I genuinely feel privileged to have the opportunity to make a difference in young people's lives.

I always say, and haven't ever meant it in a cliché way – **teaching is the best job in the world."**

Teaching ✓

Every Lesson Shapes a Life

Milkround back with a bang for university graduates

PwC puts paid to stagnation in graduate salaries

Cat

year, more than anyone else in the private sector.

That makes how PwC is structuring its pay increase more interesting. It is raising its starting salary went from £29,000 in 2011 to all of £30,000 by 2021.

The increase in accounting and professional services hasn't been quite that bad. The industry went from an esti-

graduates through the promise of training, the name on the CV and an accounting qualification three years down the line rather than purely pay — particularly since the more money orientated

has also become a more get for firms, with the Big ever-larger numbers of and apprentices and trac nomic backgrounds in its

If those from less

Hiring up a jobs marke gets a boo

DEMAND for new staf Scottish firms picked last month, a bank has sa with the jobs

---

Civil Service fast stream scrapped for a yea

Cabinet ministers object to the Prime Minister's efforts to shrink Whitehall headcount to 2016 levels

By Ben Riley-Smith POLITICAL EDITOR

the country's brightest graduates working for the Government, will not run in 2023 as part of efforts to shrink the Civil Service by a fifth.

The decision was signed off at the Cabinet Office board meeting on May 19, which was chaired by Stephen Barclay, Mr Johnson's chief of staff

were made as part of the scheme, which is seen as a fast track to senior roles in the civil service.

Most of the permanent secretaries running government departments entered via the fast stream. The scheme includes applications for the

some opposition around the table. Michael Gove, the Communities Secretary, is understood to have criticised the idea duri oversaw Senti

are also understood to have privately raised concerns about the change. However, Mr Johnson and Mr Bar

and the cost of government British people. A temporary p fast-stream recruitment will m progress in efforts to

---

Lawyers and investment bankers top rankings as UK's best paid graduates

LOUIS GOSS

LAW FIRMS are now on par with investment banks as the UK's highest paying graduate employers, according to new figures from High Fliers.

The graduate salaries paid out by Britain's major law firms are par with

cording to High Fliers figure ting them on par with invest banks (£50,000) and ahead of co ing (£47,500), oil (£40,000), and cial services companies (£38,000).

On average, graduates working the public sector received lowest salaries of £23, behind those working engineering (£28.

UK law firms nov

Market rates: Ald pays graduates as much as tech firm

Sian Griffiths
Education Editor

It may surprise parents

the levels of responsibility available and the fact that you work towards runni

---

Now students face having to repay their loans for 40 years

Criti pay plan h tax – s insist ake-up rness

will end up pay dent loans in full na that could see yments for up to

ke-up for student e, the repayment m will be extended urrent 30- hreshold will also £25,000. under the more than

No cash if you don't pass maths and English GCSEs

ments, which are subject to con spons to a

thousands. Yet the highest e who

Students knee deep in debts of over £100k

By Matthew Davis

Government decided to

SANDS of graduates have niversity with more than 00 in debts.

figures from the Student Company show 5.6 million ts past and present are in a where they face having to ack tuition and maintenance which have a combined outng balance of £161billion.

statistics also show there are than 6,000 students who managed to clock up more 100,000 in debt.

individual has a balance t their name with the SLC for ,830. There is another with ,070 of debt as well as 29 graduates with loan balances £60,000.

and bigger. Last ye per day in interest to students' loan ac

Graduates are on back the loan with 9 per cent of anyt above the annual sa which is currently £2

'The edu system is

The Institute for has calculated that students will fail to balances within 30 int the Governm

---

Britain slides into crisis

● Bank chief warns of long recession ● Interest rate rise pushes up mortgage bills ● Worst squeeze for 60 years predicted

Arthi Nachiappan, Mehreen Khan
Oliver Wright Policy Editor

Britain is heading for a protract recession as inflation surges abo 11 per cent, causing the worst sq on living standards for more tha years, the Bank of England has wa

In a drastic set of forecasts economy, the Bank said househ would suffer a record two years of incomes as the global gas pri up energy bills.

Get used to the grim

BoE warns of long recession as interest rates rise by half-point

---

Bank raises rates and warns of 13% inflation

Larry Elliott
Phillip Inman

Threadneedle Street said it had no choice but to r

to the war as he predicts

n to last 15 months ● Inflation set to hit 13% ● Worse outlook than US and

Red alert
BoE May and August forecasts for GDP growth and CPI inflat
Great-on-year (%)
GDP — May Aug CPI

Understanding the Graduate Job Market

By **Martin Birchall**
Managing Director, High Fliers Research

At the beginning of the Coronavirus crisis in March 2020, many of the UK's top employers were forced to pause or re-evaluate their graduate recruitment and many were unable to continue with that's year's planned annual intake of university-leavers.

The final number of graduates recruited by employers featured in *The Times Top 100 Graduate Employers* in 2020 was a sixth lower than had been originally intended and over 12 per cent less than in 2019.

Graduate recruitment was cut in thirteen out of fifteen industries and business sectors, most noticeably at major engineering & industrial companies and accounting & professional services firms, where over 700 planned vacancies were left unfilled.

This was the most significant annual fall in graduate recruitment since the global financial crisis of 2008 and 2009, when graduate vacancies in the UK dropped by an unprecedented 23 per cent in less than 18 months. Then, the graduate job market bounced back in 2010 with an annual increase in vacancies of more than 12 per cent, but it took a further five years for graduate recruitment to overtake the pre-recession peak recorded in 2007.

By 2019, graduate recruitment was up by 43 per cent compared to the number of vacancies available in 2009 – the low point in the graduate job market during the economic crisis – and had been expected to rise even higher in 2020 and beyond.

The Coronavirus pandemic brought this period of sustained growth to a very abrupt end. But unlike previous economic downturns and recessions, the majority of the country's best-known employers did continue with their graduate recruitment, albeit with fewer places at many organisations, rather than postponing or cutting their entry-level programmes entirely.

Graduate recruitment at the UK's top employers began to bounce back in 2021, with more entry-level vacancies on offer in nine key industries and business sectors, including technology, retail and consulting. And having made very significant cuts to their graduate recruitment in 2020, a number of employers in the engineering & industrial sector needed to step-up their next annual intake.

The overall result was that graduate recruitment increased by 9.4 per cent in 2021 and this strong growth continued into 2022 too. Over the past twelve months, graduate vacancies have risen in all fifteen key industries and business sectors represented in *The Times Top 100 Graduate Employers*, an annual increase of 15.7 per cent in the number of entry-level jobs available.

" The wider economic situation is deteriorating and this is likely to have an impact on the graduate job market over the next 18 months. "

This is the largest year-on-year rise ever for the UK's leading graduate employers and took graduate recruitment to its highest level yet, 11 per cent higher than the pre-pandemic peak in graduate recruitment recorded in 2019. The 'V-shaped' recovery in the graduate job market largely mirrors the recovery in the wider economy.

But with the UK now expected to fall into recession during the 2022-2023 academic year, the wider economic situation is deteriorating and this is likely to have an impact on the graduate job market over the next eighteen months.

At the outset of the new recruitment season, the graduate employers listed in *The Times Top 100 Graduate Employers* are predicting that they will have a total of 26,428 graduate vacancies for autumn 2023 start dates.

Although this is 6 per cent fewer than the number of university-leavers recruited in 2022, the fall in graduate vacancies year-on-year is limited to just two individual employment sectors.

Within the public sector, the 'pausing' of the Civil Service Fast Steam in 2023 means a reduction of almost 1,000 graduate roles, compared with the opportunities available in 2022. And in the accountancy & professional services sector, having

under-recruited at the start of the pandemic in 2020, the leading firms stepped-up their trainee recruitment significantly in both 2021 and 2022. As a result, graduate vacancies at the 'Big Four' professional services firms are expected to return to pre-pandemic levels this year.

In the other thirteen out of fifteen key industries and business sectors, graduate recruitment is predicted to rise or match 2022 recruitment levels in the next 12 months, with the strongest growth expected at the ten engineering & industrial employers featured in this year's rankings.

Overall, a quarter of the UK's top employers are planning to hire more graduates in 2023, over half think they will match their previous intake, but a sixth of organisations are likely to recruit fewer university-leavers over the coming year.

Employers in the investment banking and legal sectors remain the most consistent graduate recruiters, having made no cuts to their recruitment in 2020 and maintained their graduate vacancies in 2021 and 2022 at levels that match the sectors' pre-pandemic recruitment.

Despite the reduction in their recruitment, the largest number of graduate vacancies in 2023 is expected to be at the accounting & professional

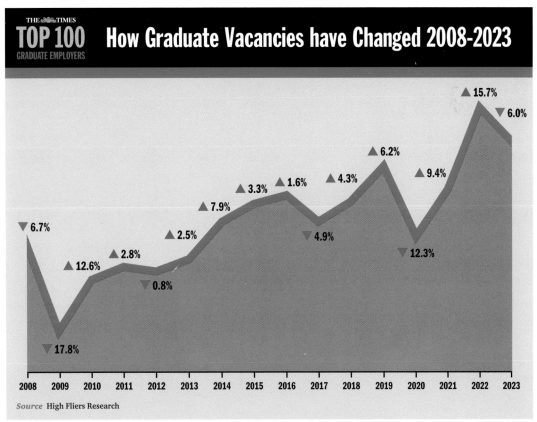

How Graduate Vacancies have Changed 2008-2023

Source High Fliers Research

firms and public sector employers, with a total of more than 9,800 entry-level positions available for new graduates.

The two employers from *The Times Top 100 Graduate Employers* with the biggest graduate recruitment targets for 2023 are the accounting & professional services firm PwC – which is aiming to recruit 1,800 new trainees in the year ahead – and Teach First, the popular programme that recruits new graduates to teach in schools in low income communities around the UK, has 1,750 places available.

Other very substantial individual graduate recruiters in 2023 include online retailer Amazon (1,300 vacancies), the accounting & professional services firms Deloitte, EY and KPMG (1,000 graduate vacancies each), technology firm Kubrick (900 vacancies) and Enterprise, the car & van rental company (800 vacancies).

Three-fifths of *Top 100* employers have vacancies for graduates in technology, over half have opportunities in finance, and more than a third are recruiting for general management vacancies, human resources roles, engineering positions, or sales and marketing jobs.

A fifth of the country's top graduate employers are looking for new recruits to work in research & development, but there are fewer graduate jobs

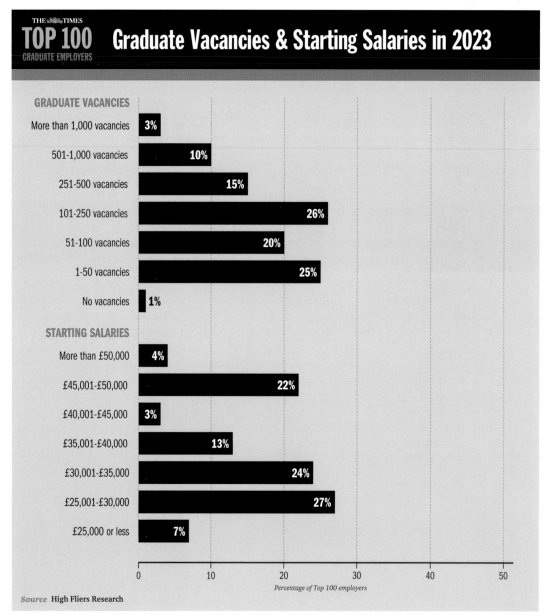

THE TIMES
TOP 100 **Graduate Vacancies & Starting Salaries in 2023**
GRADUATE EMPLOYERS

GRADUATE VACANCIES

- More than 1,000 vacancies — 3%
- 501-1,000 vacancies — 10%
- 251-500 vacancies — 15%
- 101-250 vacancies — 26%
- 51-100 vacancies — 20%
- 1-50 vacancies — 25%
- No vacancies — 1%

STARTING SALARIES

- More than £50,000 — 4%
- £45,001-£50,000 — 22%
- £40,001-£45,000 — 3%
- £35,001-£40,000 — 13%
- £30,001-£35,000 — 24%
- £25,001-£30,000 — 27%
- £25,000 or less — 7%

Percentage of Top 100 employers

Source **High Fliers Research**

Become a
problem solver
for the planet

We're constantly seeking innovative
thinkers who challenge everything,
to build a world they want to be part of.

Join us and improve quality of life.

ARCADIS

available in retailing or in more specialist areas, such as logistics & supply chain, purchasing, property and the media.

Four-fifths of *Top 100* employers have graduate vacancies in London in 2023, and half have posts available elsewhere in the south east of England. Up to half also have roles in the north west of England, the south west, the Midlands, Yorkshire and the north east. Over two-fifths are recruiting for graduate roles in Scotland, but Northern Ireland, Wales and East Anglia have the fewest employers with vacancies this year.

Graduate starting salaries at the UK's leading employers have changed little over the last decade – rising by just £1,000 between 2012 and 2021 – but went up by £2,000 in 2022 to a median salary of £32,000, the first annual increase for seven years.

The highest starting salaries for the 'Class of 2023' are expected to be at the leading investment banks & fund managers and law firms (each offering a median of £50,000) and consulting firms (£47,500).

A quarter of employers featured in *The Times Top 100 Graduate Employers* are now offering starting salaries of more than £45,000 for their new recruits. The most generous salaries publicised within this edition are at the NatWest Group, which is paying new graduates up to £60,000, and law

firm White & Case, which is offering new trainees a salary of £52,000 in 2023. Rival law firms Clifford Chance, Linklaters, Slaughter and May, Freshfields Bruckhaus Deringer, Baker McKenzie, Latham & Watkins and Reed Smith each have graduate starting salaries of £50,000.

Consulting firm Newton and technology company TPP also have graduate packages worth up to £50,000, whilst retailer Aldi continues to pay a sector-leading graduate starting salary of £44,000, plus a fully expensed company car.

A third of the UK's leading employers now recruit graduates year-round, or in different phases during the year, and will accept applications throughout the 2022-2023 recruitment season until all their vacancies are filled. For employers with an annual application deadline, most are in November or December, although a limited number have October or post-Christmas deadlines for their graduate programmes.

So there is every incentive to apply early for the graduate vacancies available in 2023. And whilst the economic prospects for the UK may be increasingly uncertain, the organisations featured in *The Times Top 100 Graduate Employers* are expecting to offer a near-record number of entry-level vacancies for university-leavers and a wide range of opportunities in different industries and business sectors.

TOP 100 Graduate Vacancies at Top 100 Employers in 2023

	2021		GRADUATE VACANCIES IN 2023	% CHANGE IN 2023	% CHANGE IN 2022	MEDIAN STARTING SALARY IN 2023
1.	1	ACCOUNTANCY & PROFESSIONAL SERVICES FIRMS	6,075	▼ 11.4%	▲ 25.9%	£32,000
2.	2	PUBLIC SECTOR EMPLOYERS	3,720	▼ 21.7%	▲ 2.5%	£22,400
3.	3	TECHNOLOGY COMPANIES	3,100	▲ 4.2%	▲ 38.9%	£32,000
4.	5	ENGINEERING & INDUSTRIAL COMPANIES	2,510	▲ 18.4%	▲ 19.0%	£29,000
5.	4	INVESTMENT BANKS & FUND MANAGERS	2,320	▲ 2.9%	▲ 2.9%	£50,000
6.	7	RETAILERS	1,916	▲ 9.0%	▲ 12.3%	£36,500
7.	6	BANKING & FINANCIAL SERVICES	1,790	▲ 0.6%	▲ 18.9%	£40,000
8.	8	ARMED FORCES	1,100	NO CHANGE	▲ 1.9%	£28,900
9.	9	LAW FIRMS	1,037	▲ 3.5%	▲ 1.4%	£50,000
10.	10	MEDIA ORGANISATIONS	920	▲ 4.0%	▲ 15.3%	£33,000
11.	11	CONSULTING FIRMS	485	▲ 5.4%	▲ 27.0%	£47,500
12.	12	CONSUMER GOODS MANUFACTURERS	190	▲ 7.3%	▲ 11.4%	£32,000
13.	14	OIL & ENERGY COMPANIES	170	▲ 23.2%	▲ 38.0%	£42,500
14.	15	PROPERTY	150	▲ 15.4%	▲ 4.0%	£26,500
15.	13	CHEMICAL & PHARMACEUTICAL COMPANIES	145	▲ 0.7%	▲ 14.3%	£31,000

Source High Fliers Research

How will you navigate our world, your way?

At EY, our purpose is building a better working world. The insights and services we provide help to create long-term value for clients, people, and society.

We empower our people with the right mindsets and skills to navigate what's next, become the transformative leaders the world needs, pursue careers as unique as they are, and build their own exceptional EY experiences.

Working across 150 countries within four business areas: Assurance, Consulting, Strategy and Transactions, and Tax. Our teams work at the cutting edge, drawing upon fresh thinking and advanced technology to help make better business decisions. You'll have the scope, support, and challenges to unleash your potential.

We have opportunities available for:

- ▸ Work experience

- ▸ Apprenticeships

- ▸ Summer internship and industrial placement programmes

- ▸ Graduate programmes

Find out more and apply today:
ey.com/uk/students

The exceptional EY experience. It's yours to build.

■ ■ ■

**The better the question. The better the answer.
The better the world works.**

EY

**Building a better
working world**

Everyday Amazing.

GET READY FOR MORE

GRADUATE AREA MANAGER PROGRAMME

- £44,000 starting salary (rising to £81,415 in year five) • Pension • Healthcare
- Fully expensed company car • All-year round recruitment but places fill quickly

There's many reasons to join our Graduate Area Manager programme: the responsibility, the exposure, the support...and yes, the salary and the car. But top of your list should be the opportunity to get involved, give more – and get even more back. At Aldi, you'll progress at pace (just like our tills). With drive and determination you'll go from time in store to managing your own £multi-million business and leading your team to success. Depending on business needs, graduates with the willingness and drive to be flexible in both their areas of responsibility and location may get the chance to take on an exciting project role. If you've got the enthusiasm and the ambition, don't shop around – this is your chance to become a future leader at Aldi.

aldirecruitment.co.uk/graduates

ALDI MEANS MORE

Successful Graduate Job Hunting

By **Elizabeth Darlington**
Director of Careers, London School of Economics and Political Science

S tudents graduating from university over the past two years have not only had to cope with the huge disruption that the Coronavirus pandemic wreaked on their studies and university life, but also dramatic changes to the recruitment process for their first graduate job too.

Few, if any, of the country's best-known employers have been able to take part in on-campus recruitment events since the start of the pandemic, and almost all of the usual promotions and publicity for their graduate programmes were moved online instead. And at most organisations, the assessment process for applicants has been fully virtual too, with even the final round of selection for new graduates completed remotely.

Happily, many of these on-campus recruitment promotions and the in-person aspects of the graduate assessment process will be returning for the 2022-2023 academic year. Whether it's university careers fairs, skills sessions, careers talks or face-to-face recruitment interviews, we know how much students have missed the buzz of being in the same room as their future employers and having the chance to meet recent graduates or talk directly to graduate recruiters – things that have been hard to replicate online.

These events aren't just about finding out more about different graduate programmes or gathering information – for many students it's an important way to build their confidence, practise networking with prospective employers, and develop more of the inter-personal skills that recruiters are looking for. It's often also an essential way to discover the culture and 'feel' of an organisation and its employees.

For the year ahead, universities are working hard to give students as many opportunities as possible to engage in-person with graduate employers, but there will be some differences to the events and promotions that ran before the pandemic.

Some universities will be offering large-scale careers fairs, whereas others will focus on smaller sector-based events, as well as employer-led skills and networking events, alongside a programme of employers' own on-campus recruitment presentations.

With most universities expecting a full 'return to normal' to campus and academic life in 2022-2023, many students will be able to come straight from their lectures, seminars and tutorials to these on-campus recruitment events and promotions.

But many events are likely to include an online option too, so that students who aren't able to attend in-person can still participate. And not all employers are planning to return to in-person promotions yet, opting to continue instead

THE TIMES TOP 100 GRADUATE EMPLOYERS

❝ If you've spent fifteen minutes on an employer's website and you're bored senseless, then it's probably not the job for you. ❞

Embrace change.
Invent the future.
Rethinkers wanted.

dyson

careers.dyson.com/early-careers

with their 'online first' approach to graduate recruitment.

For today's undergraduates who are just starting to think about their career options and graduate job options, then the outlook is encouraging – the graduate job market has already bounced-back strongly from the impact of the pandemic and a number of employers featured in *The Times Top 100 Graduate Employers* are expecting to recruit a record number of new graduates in 2023.

If you're in your first year, then as well as making new friends, getting to know your course and settling into university, now is also the time to start doing some of the things which will help you gain and develop the professional skills that employers are looking for.

Joining student societies, taking part in mentoring programmes, or doing extracurricular things that you love – whether that's rock-climbing, amateur theatre, playing sport or doing charity work – will all show who you really are as an individual, what makes you 'tick' and what you really enjoy outside of your studies. So too will taking a part-time job during term-time or doing voluntary work.

Each of these experiences will enable employers to see how these different parts of your life make you a three-dimensional person, not just another graduate who's studied a familiar degree at a well-known university. It's about picking things you like and are interested in, and then doing them well.

A key part of these initial steps is also to take time to reflect on what you experience. We get so many students who come into the careers service who say they've not done anything relevant or anything that an employer would be interested in. Whereas in reality, they've actually done plenty of things that recruiters would certainly value, it's just that they aren't able to talk about their experiences in an energising way because they've not considered what they've learnt or the skills they've developed.

Your first year is also a great time to begin doing some initial research into the kinds of careers that you might be interested in. Make time to visit your university careers service and discover the resources it offers – both within the careers service itself and online. And look out too for the different introductory experiences that are on on-offer from a wide range of graduate employers, such as taster courses, open days and spring weeks. Even if you arrived at university with a clear idea of the career you'd like to pursue, we'd always recommend keeping your options open and explore what else is out there.

When you reach the penultimate year of your degree, that's the time to try and arrange formal work experience with graduate employers. This is another aspect of graduate job hunting that was significantly disrupted by the pandemic – very few employers were able to offer their usual summer internships in the summers of 2020 or 2021, with many opting for virtual internships instead.

At most major graduate employers, in-person work experience for students and recent graduates returned in the summer of 2022. Getting a place on an 8-10 week paid summer internship can be a highly competitive process and many employers expect students to apply during the autumn of their penultimate year for a work placement the following summer.

As well as being a great way to build up your experience of a particular type of job or business sector, a successful internship can also lead to an offer of a graduate job with the employer, particularly for roles in accountancy, law, investment banking and other careers in finance.

Alternatively, if you're thinking about a career in the creative industries, for example, spending your summer working freelance to build up a portfolio of experiences can be just as valuable. Or you might decide that you just want to have a long break over the summer, rather than look into your career preparations and, of course, that's fine too, but be prepared that you may get questions from employers about how you spent your time.

Once you reach your final year and are making job applications to employers, then it's time to think through your strategy and start preparing for the assessment and selection processes that most of the major graduate employers use.

Employers are looking for applicants who can demonstrate they've researched and understood the roles and programmes they're offering. That's difficult if you cast your net too wide and attempt to apply to graduate employers in lots of different industries or business sectors. You're more likely to be successful if you pick two or three related sectors and then look at three or four organisations within them. It's almost always more effective to make a smaller number of higher quality applications, rather than rush through dozens of applications to employers you know little about.

Make full use of companies' websites to do your initial research and listen to your instincts. If you've spent fifteen minutes on an employer's site reading their stuff and you're bored senseless, then it's probably not the job for you.

When you find an employer you are interested in, try and get in touch with somebody from the organisation. It doesn't need to be someone senior, a recent alumnus from your university would be an ideal person to speak to. LinkedIn can be really helpful for this and if you can set up an informal coffee or a chat over Zoom, you'll learn a great deal, above and beyond the employer's 'official' recruitment messages.

On one level, this can help you understand whether you're really interested in the organisation and, if you are, it can give you invaluable information and insight that you can use when you're writing your application or getting ready for an interview.

Once you've submitted your applications, then you'll need to prepare for the testing stage of the graduate recruitment process. Most of the largest employers use numeracy tests, psychometric tests and other ability tests as their knockout round for applicants.

Your university careers service can help you understand what these tests will involve and will help you prepare and practise for them. In particular, if you've not done maths since your GCSE, you may need to work on getting it back up to a reasonable standard.

The next stage is likely to be an online recorded interview, where you'll be asked a series of questions about your motivation and skills & abilities. The good news is that employers generally ask very similar questions during these timed interviews, so you should be able to research your responses in advance and feel confident that you're going to give good, detailed answers to each of the questions.

You'll be up against a countdown clock for each answer and you'll need to make full use of the time available, to put across as much information as possible. It's a tricky thing to do because you're not interacting with a real interviewer who can ask you more about something you've just said.

Careers advisers at your careers service can help you prepare and rehearse your answers – and many provide access to online platforms for mock interviews that give you feedback and the chance to watch your interviews back.

This can be a very beneficial way to reflect on how you look and seem during an interview and if you come across as self-assured or nervous. You can also ask your family and friends to assist with this too. They can be a big help in terms of checking if you're answering questions fully

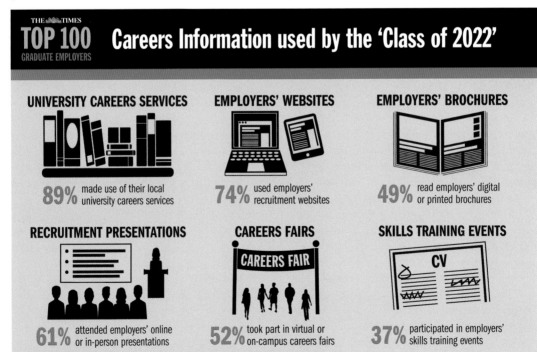

We want to make
a difference to people's lives,
including yours.

Find out just how many opportunities we
have for an amazing and rewarding career.

enough or if you're repeating the same answer to different questions.

However you do it, practising for interviews is one of the most important skills you can develop for the graduate selection process – and will give you the confidence you need when you come to do interviews with employers that you really want to work for.

The final selection round is likely to be an assessment centre with the employer, but it may not be clear when you apply whether it will be done in-person or as a virtual experience. Regardless of how these are conducted, there are likely to be similar elements, such as group exercises, presentations, and individual interviews. It's important to get practise each of these beforehand, because they may well be very unfamiliar to you. And you should prepare separately for in-person and online selections – it's very different performing in a group activity when you're on Zoom, compared to taking part in person.

Despite the increasing number of graduate vacancies available, competition for places on the most sought-after graduate programmes remains very fierce. It's sensible, therefore, to have a 'plan B', in case you don't get the job offer or offers

you're hoping for. The reality is that you may have to be flexible about your options in an increasingly fluid employment market. Employers' recruitment needs are changing very quickly at the moment and if you're unwilling to compromise about the sector or industry you join after university, you could find yourself without anything to go onto at all.

Your alternative plan still needs to excite you and interest you, as well as developing and stretching you and giving you good experience for the future. But it doesn't have to be anything other than a first job – you shouldn't feel under pressure to find something that will be right for life. Concentrate on finding something you'll enjoy for a period, where you'll be learning, networking and looking out for the next opportunity that interests you – whether that takes a few months or a few years.

Finally, when you're considering a graduate job offer – or you're in the fortunate position to have more than one offer – think carefully about whether the employer is offering the community and sense of belonging that you're looking for. Ask yourself, 'can I see myself working there, can I see myself working with these people?' and if the answer is a unequivocal 'yes' then you've almost certainly found an employer that's right for you.

THE TIMES TOP 100 GRADUATE EMPLOYERS

How the 'Class of 2022' Applied for Graduate Jobs

WORK EXPERIENCE

Two-fifths of students who did internships or work placements at university received a **graduate job offer** from the employer they worked for

JOB APPLICATIONS IN FINAL YEAR

Graduates made an average of **13 job applications** each, during their final year at university.

SELECTION & ASSESSMENT

3 out of **4** graduate job hunters found employers' online tests and recorded video interviews **difficult**

GRADUATE JOB OFFERS

A **third** of graduates from the 'Class of 2022' received at least one **graduate job offer** before leaving university

Source **High Fliers Research** 12,432 final year students leaving UK universities in the summer of 2022 were asked about the job applications they had made to graduate employers and their progress with job offers, during interviews for *The UK Graduate Careers Survey 2022*

More than just glasses

You'll know us for one thing but we're so much more. Find out just how many opportunities we have for an amazing and rewarding career.

Life-changing.
For you.
And potentially millions.

When you work for the NHS, it's about making a difference. Not just for you and your journey, but for millions of patients and their families and communities.

Graduate Management Training Scheme

The NHS Graduate Management Training Scheme offers you a fast track to a senior non-clinical role. It's your opportunity to get on-the-job training and experience, post-graduate qualifications, early leadership responsibility and a strong support network. Not to mention building a far-reaching professional network with 249 other graduate trainees.

With placements across England in a variety of hospital and office settings, you could be improving patient care, developing better ways to use data, creating new strategies and much more.

Your days will be challenging but exceptionally rewarding. And every day you'll move towards becoming a healthcare leader of the future who can effect powerful change.

 NHSGradScheme

 NHSGraduateScheme

 nhsgraduatescheme

 NHS Graduate Management Training Scheme (GMTS)

 NHS Graduate Management Training Scheme

THE TIMES
GRADUATE RECRUITMENT
AWARDS 2022
'Graduate Employer of Choice'
GENERAL MANAGEMENT

THE TIMES
GRADUATE RECRUITMENT
AWARDS 2022
'Graduate Employer of Choice'
HUMAN RESOURCES

Start your journey here

Visit: www.graduates.nhs.uk

Preparing for the New World of Work

By **Jonathan Black**

Director, Careers Service & Internship Office, University of Oxford

As a final year student, or recent graduate, you've spent most of your recent life studying and, to some extent, considering the next step into the world of work.

Whether you've known for a long time, or you still don't know quite what you want to do, what is work going to be like in 2023 and beyond? What would you like it to be and what will you actually find? How much choice do you have and how close will it be to your dream?

The culture of the organisation where you choose to work is going to sit somewhere on a range. At one end of the range, the company will expect you to turn up at specific times, do as you're told, stay all day, and come into the place of work every day.

At the other end of the range, they'll welcome you bringing your "authentic self" to work, listen to and welcome your views, act on your opinions, provide work that has real meaning and purpose for you, and let you work from home/anywhere, coming into the office once or twice a month.

Organisations are still working out where on this spectrum they want to and actually can be, and even by summer 2023 it's unlikely that the balance they alight on will be the final position.

For example, technology continues to evolve, making online meetings and hybrid working more effective – and we too are all adapting our ways of working to make online more efficient.

But the pandemic and lockdown also showed us that while we can be efficient at basic processes and operations when working alone, from home, strategy and team creativity are not nearly as easy online, and fundamentally we miss the social side of work. There is also benefit to a physical separation of home and work, that can help us switch off work, relax and recharge.

THE TIMES TOP 100 GRADUATE EMPLOYERS

❝ Three out of four new graduates said it was important they should be based in an office, rather than at home. ❞

New ways of working, and where to operate on that range of 'work from home' to 'full time in the office' are being reviewed not just for new starters, but also the recent joiners, mid-career, and senior staff as well.

People who've been at the organisation for many years have already built their networks and may not feel they need to be in the office or onsite as much, whereas you, as a new starter, would want to meet them in work for the social and informal learning.

This last point is not trivial. The latest survey of final year students from the 'Class of 2022', produced by High Fliers Research, reported that the top priority for new graduates was 'having a good social life through work', something that two-fifths of new graduates described as being 'very important'.

Lisa Dell'Avvocato, Group Lead of Emerging Talent Strategy at Lloyds Banking Group has seen this first hand. "We know a big reason people want to start a graduate programme is to make new friends, we're already seeing a rise in people taking on the role of social secretary," she observes.

Graduates with caring responsibilities, or those who have a long commute, or have distant clients all need to be accommodated as well. Your future employer is also wanting to consider challenges on sustainability, governance, and equality, and all while staying profitable. Layer on top of these, rising inflation and slowing economic growth worldwide, increased costs of doing business (such as the extra bureaucracy, costs and delays caused by Brexit) and the challenges of recruiting at all levels, will all make an interesting time over the next few years in business.

And then all this rather depends on the type of work you're going to do. How many days a week in the office is not something you can choose if, for example, you're in school teaching, social work, healthcare, manufacturing, uniformed services, hospitality, tourism, or retail.

The same survey from High Fliers Research reported that almost three out of four new graduates said it was important they should be 'based in an office or at an employer's site, rather than at home' when they start work, with a third stating it was 'very important' to them. Just one in six said it was a key priority for them to be able to work from home.

Graduate employers are responding to this. Louise Farrar, former Director of Talent Acquisition at PwC, said "the firm has made it very clear that staff will be in the office 2-3 days a week." She explained that the firm considers in-person work to be important for, "networking, collaboration, and peer learning – none of which is the same online."

At KPMG, Kevin Hogarth, Chief People Officer, agreed that "there is value in coming to the office," and the firm has set this at the moment at two days per week. He added that when staff are in, they want the work to be, "purposeful, for example in team meetings, or group training," and the firm has introduced Apps so teams can book desks near each other in the collaborative open-plan shared space.

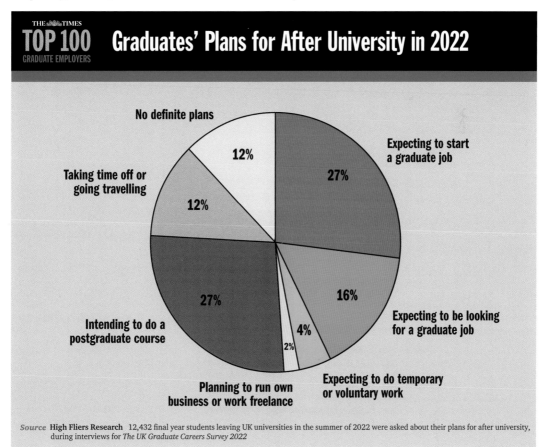

THE TIMES
TOP 100 Graduates' Plans for After University in 2022
GRADUATE EMPLOYERS

- No definite plans — 12%
- Expecting to start a graduate job — 27%
- Taking time off or going travelling — 12%
- Intending to do a postgraduate course — 27%
- Planning to run own business or work freelance — 2%
- 4%
- Expecting to be looking for a graduate job — 16%
- Expecting to do temporary or voluntary work

Source **High Fliers Research** 12,432 final year students leaving UK universities in the summer of 2022 were asked about their plans for after university, during interviews for *The UK Graduate Careers Survey 2022*

Dell'Avvocato agrees too. "New ways of working will improve the experience with us ... including better technology, and spaces to collaborate and make connections," she says.

Beyond the question of where and when you'll be working – both of which are likely to evolve – the cultural aspects of your workplace will also be important. As you explore and select the organisation to join, and where you'll spend the majority of your waking hours, you'd be well-advised to explore the culture of the organisation. As it's hard to capture 'culture' accurately in brochures or on web sites, you can do this best by chatting to current staff and, with due caution, checking out Glassdoor and social media.

At PwC, they're interviewing online, and then

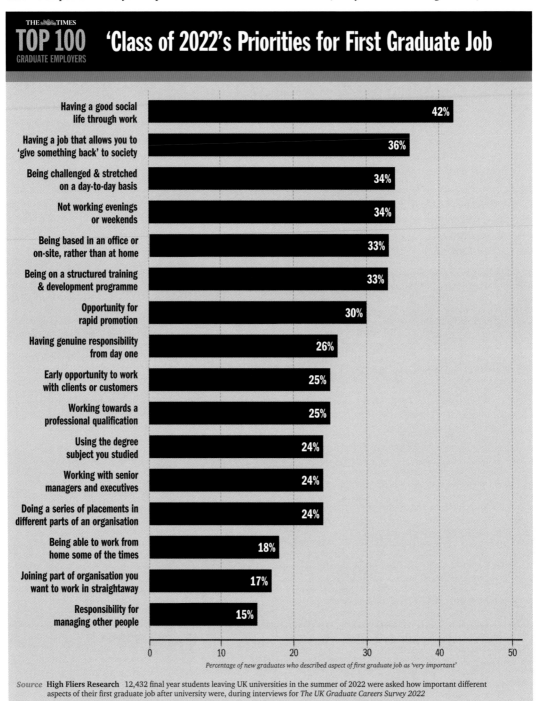

THE TIMES
TOP 100 'Class of 2022's Priorities for First Graduate Job
GRADUATE EMPLOYERS

Priority	Percentage
Having a good social life through work	42%
Having a job that allows you to 'give something back' to society	36%
Being challenged & stretched on a day-to-day basis	34%
Not working evenings or weekends	34%
Being based in an office or on-site, rather than at home	33%
Being on a structured training & development programme	33%
Opportunity for rapid promotion	30%
Having genuine responsibility from day one	26%
Early opportunity to work with clients or customers	25%
Working towards a professional qualification	25%
Using the degree subject you studied	24%
Working with senior managers and executives	24%
Doing a series of placements in different parts of an organisation	24%
Being able to work from home some of the times	18%
Joining part of organisation you want to work in straightaway	17%
Responsibility for managing other people	15%

Percentage of new graduates who described aspect of first graduate job as 'very important'

Source **High Fliers Research** 12,432 final year students leaving UK universities in the summer of 2022 were asked how important different aspects of their first graduate job after university were, during interviews for *The UK Graduate Careers Survey 2022*

Big on ambition.
Even bigger on opportunities.

If you've got the drive, we've got the journey. Build skills and confidence on our graduate programmes and discover what it takes to be part of something great. An operation that feeds the nation.

A career a lidl less ordinary.

 lidlcareers.co.uk

inviting offer-holders to visit the offices – that's a great opportunity to get the feel of the place and your potential future colleagues. If other employers don't offer this, you can always ask to do it once you hold an offer.

With senior staff rather enjoying the freedom of working from home, how will you as a new graduate get enough face time with experienced colleagues?

The old, quasi-apprenticeship model of learning your trade at the feet of the master has been disrupted by the pandemic. Everyone seems to agree that informal and in person conversations are an effective form of on-the-job learning. Sitting in client meetings and observing how senior colleagues run events and present difficult or complex issues is much more realistic than online observation or even reading about it.

Organisations are still exploring the best way to combine this informal teaching with working from home/anywhere policies.

At PwC, they encourage teams to decide for themselves when to come to the office together; of course, one of the benefits of large organisations is the chance to meet people in different teams, working on different topics with other clients. Building those networks goes rather better in person and at social events.

At Hachette, the trade and professional publishers, eight employee networks have been created so staff can be part of a group not related to work, but to their interests and beliefs. David Shelley, CEO of Hachette UK, describes these groups as hugely important. If you worked there, you could be involved in networks on LGBTQ+, gender balance, wellbeing, BAME, multi-faith, age and more – there's a lobbying and feedback element to these too so you'd get your voice heard in the organisation.

Employers featured in *The Times Top 100 Graduate Employers* are acutely conscious of environment, sustainability and governance (ESG) – and equality, diversity, and inclusivity (EDI) issues. Many have appointed champions of these topics to jump start the efforts of the organisation in those areas – of course, ideally ESG and EDI would be mainstreamed into everyone's role and not implicitly delegated to a particular person.

This might be where you could make your mark at your new employer. As Dell'Avvocato says: "there are many roles across the Group that play an active role in supporting the transition to a low carbon economy, so graduates will be able to actively get involved and support the work we do."

As you assess your potential employer, you could check that it is open to your questions on the topics that matter to you. This might be sustainability, diversity, support for LGBTQ+, mentoring, faith, and the training that's available.

And it's not just the answers to your questions, but whether they are open to the discussion. Just in case the worst happens, what's their approach to handling harassment or bullying – is there an anonymous helpline for example?

Hogarth observes that at KPMG, staff are wanting to learn about the firm's position on broader topics such as ESG, Net Zero, equality and so on. He says that candidates are asking more questions about these important topics, and that they expect to hear honest answers.

Farrar at PwC agrees – they are seeing staff seeking to understand the values of the firm, such as how they choose clients for example. And at Clifford Chance, Laura Yeates, Head of Graduate Talent, describes the open and challenging questions that students on the firm's Vacation Scheme are asking of senior partners.

In order to attract 'Generation Z' talent – that's you, if you were born between 1997 and 2012 – employers, particularly those in *The Times Top 100 Graduate Employers*, realise they have to adapt to attract and retain you.

When you enter the world of work in 2023, or in the years that follow, you'll find an open workplace, where discussion is welcomed, where employers recognise that work is about much more than the tasks you are set and where you can flourish with your "whole self," with your non-work interests playing a vital part of who you are.

Employers are still evolving the details of where and when you'll be working, but the balance has shifted from measuring only input to some more measure of output – trusting you to dress and conduct yourself appropriately, be a good ambassador for the organisation, and work at the best time for you as long as you get the work done effectively.

After graduation, you may not get everything you seek immediately, but the first job in the world of work is a stepping-stone on the path of your future career. You can get more choice and control as you progress – but seek a good role that would give you intellectual challenge, interesting work, and a good social life within work.

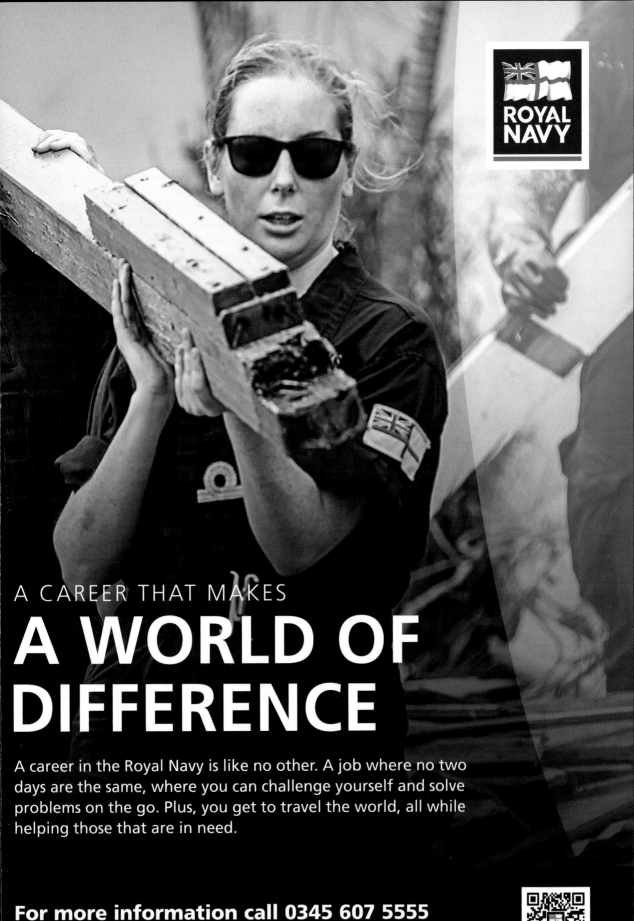

A CAREER THAT MAKES
A WORLD OF DIFFERENCE

A career in the Royal Navy is like no other. A job where no two days are the same, where you can challenge yourself and solve problems on the go. Plus, you get to travel the world, all while helping those that are in need.

For more information call 0345 607 5555
Visit royalnavy.mod.uk/careers

TAKE YOUR FIRST STEP INTO CONSULTING.

Get the support you need to do more from day one. Work with experts in a high-performing team. Take on complex challenges and deliver solutions that make a real change. Build your career by working in a variety of sectors and industries. Together, let's make a greater impact. Let's start doing.

To find out if a career in consulting is right for you, search **Newton Graduate Careers or visit WorkatNewton.com**

NEWTON

Kian, Operations Consultant

Your promotion

Discover how our graduates can become **managers in just two years**

Unbelievable right? Not here! You see, because our graduates enjoy so much exposure to the different parts of our business and experience so much training, they're able to progress in super-quick time. Work hard and you could even make manager in two years. And because we strive to promote from within, you'll never be short of your next opportunity in the longer-term either.

**Get started now at
careers.enterprise.co.uk**

Graduate Lives

Interviews by **Martin Birchall**

TOP 100 GRADUATE EMPLOYERS

Telling the stories of today's graduates – from their time at university, to working for Britain's top employers.

Become part of our story

Clyde & Co has grown to become a
leading global law firm in our core
sectors. With a headcount of over
5,000 staff operating from over
60 offices and associated offices
across six continents, we offer a
comprehensive range of legal services
and advice to businesses operating
at the heart of global trade and
commerce.

ARMED FORCES

Making waves as an engineering graduate

It was a childhood holiday in Devon that first inspired Lieutenant Henry Trutch to pursue a career as an officer in the Royal Navy.

I was 15 and went on holiday with my family to Dartmouth, which is home to the Britannia Royal Naval College," explains Trutch. "It's where all the Royal Navy's new officers are trained and I saw them up on the hill, marching around, and it made me wonder if it was something I could do."

He applied soon after to the Royal Navy through his local recruitment office and, having passed the Admiralty Interview Board to become a future weapons engineer, he was offered a place at the Armed Forces' own sixth form boarding college.

"I studied STEM subjects for my A-levels and went on to the University of Southampton to study electronic engineering," Trutch continues. "I was sponsored throughout my degree course by the Navy, which meant I did a training evening each week and took part in exercises and adventurous training days in return for an annual bursary."

After graduating in the summer of 2017, Trutch returned to Dartmouth for his officer training. "It was about thirty weeks, split into two phases, that took you from being a civilian into the military," he remembers. "After that, I had another year of specialist training at HMS Collingwood in Fareham, preparing to become a weapons engineer."

Trutch's first posting was to HMS Montrose, a Type 23 frigate deployed in the Gulf. "I'd done some of my training on the ship and they were an amazing team, so I was lucky they asked me back," he explains.

"I was a sub-lieutenant, directly responsible for thirty engineers in the weapons engineering department, conducting anti-piracy and maritime security operations out there."

He also had a role as a boarding officer, searching ships or boats that

HENRY TRUTCH

Lieutenant Henry Trutch, Royal Navy

had been intercepted. "We worked with the Royal Marines – they would go aboard and secure the vessel and then we would come behind to conduct the search. It's something you don't expect to do as a graduate engineer," he continues.

It proved to be an exciting posting for Trutch. "We were on patrol when the US carried out a drone strike on an Iranian general, so we spent several days on high alert protecting UK and American ships in the Gulf," he recalls.

"And we were there when the Iranian Revolutionary Guard tried to intercept the British Heritage oil tanker. We positioned ourselves in between the multiple gunboats and the tanker, in order to stop it being boarded."

Trutch worked on a four-month on, four-month off rotation for two years and was in the Gulf when the pandemic began. "We were stuck at sea for extended periods, but we tried to generate our own fun," he explains. "We had flight-deck cinemas, sporting events, barbeques

and quizzes. And lots of people learnt how to be a barber because you couldn't go ashore for a haircut."

In August 2021, Trutch returned to Portsmouth to join the UK Maritime Battle Staff as information manager. "It's a very different role for me to my previous one, but a really interesting one," he says.

"We're in charge of the NATO Response Force this year, so we're at 48-hours' notice to go anywhere NATO wants us to go. We did a big exercise earlier this year which had twenty-five warships from eleven nations and my team were responsible for pushing and pulling all the information between them."

Within the Royal Navy, officers typically move into new roles every eighteen months to two years, with the opportunity for promotion at different intervals during a career that can last as long as forty years.

"In ten years' time, I'm aiming to become a Commander weapons engineer," says Trutch. "Serving on one of our flagships, like HMS Queen Elizabeth or HMS Prince of Wales."

Lewis Rowley, Slaughter and May

LAW

At the legal cutting edge

When Lewis Rowley left school in the summer of 2014 he was all set to become an officer in the Army, but he's now a corporate lawyer at one of the City's top law firms.

Rowley had been offered a place at the Royal Military Academy Sandhurst and awarded an Army scholarship to study at university.

"A career in the military is not always a lifetime thing," he explains "So, I knew I wanted to study something that would give me flexibility and future options when I came out the other side."

He chose law at the University of Birmingham and was commissioned as a Second Lieutenant in the Army Reserve in the summer of his first year. But towards the end of his degree, he had a change of direction.

"I was working really hard and had put so much time and effort into my degree and thought, 'why not put this to good use after university?'," Rowley recalls. "I'd met people from various City law firms and thought a career in law sounded like an exciting place to start working life."

He applied for summer vacation schemes run by several top City firms – one of the main ways that law firms recruit their new trainees – but his applications weren't successful.

"I was quite disillusioned with the way it works," he remembers. "Many firms have a convoluted selection process where you fill in a lengthy application form, then do a series of online tasks and tests, before you finally get to speak to a human being at the very end of the process."

When it came to applying for a training contract, Slaughter and May's process stood out for taking a different approach. "It's very straightforward and initially requires a covering letter where you explain in brief terms why you think you'd like to work for the firm and why you might be a good fit," Rowley explains.

"Although the firm gets thousands and thousands of these letters each year, they are all read and those who are shortlisted are invited for an interview day," he continues.

Rowley was successful and was offered a training contract by Slaughter and May. The contract included completing the six-month Accelerated Legal Practice Course (now the course to prepare for the solicitors' qualifying exams) at the BPP law school in London, and then two years of full-time training at the firm.

"The training is usually divided into four six-month 'seats' in different teams, to give you as much experience as possible of the kind of work that the firm does," says Rowley.

He completed seats in the competition, financing and corporate groups, and then did a client secondment for his final six months. "By the end of my training, I'd opted to qualify into one of the firm's corporate teams," he explains. "I chose it because I had really enjoyed my time in the group during my training contract, and thought it would give a varied and interesting diet of work."

Rowley finished his training in the summer of 2020 and is now an associate at the firm.

"My job isn't one where you just sit and do one type of work repetitively, it really does change from day to day," he explains.

"On Tuesday morning this week we closed a major transaction that had been running for the past nine months," continues Rowley. "We had a call with the other side's lawyers and other advisers engaged on the transaction to confirm that everyone was happy to proceed. Thankfully they were and the transaction completed smoothly! I then spent the afternoon on a completely different matter, drafting board materials for one of our listed clients."

Rowley admits the nature of the job means the hours can be long. "Our work is interesting and intellectually challenging and that's what I think attracts most people to this job," he enthuses.

"You're well remunerated from a very early stage in your career, and there's an understanding that it is a busy environment and sometimes you will need to work late or over the weekend," he concludes. "If you're comfortable with that, then it's a fantastic place to work."

J.P. Morgan

Choose a career with choice

We're looking for students from all majors and backgrounds to join our diverse, global team.

As a top employer in financial services, J.P. Morgan does much more than manage money. Here, you'll have more chances to continuously innovate, learn and make a positive impact for our clients, customers and communities.

We offer internships in over 12 different business areas as well as Early Insight Programs to introduce you to the industry and our company.

jpmorgan.com/careers

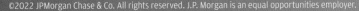

Biko | Automated Trading   **Susan** | Strategy Associate   **Ami** | Equity Research Associate

To infinity . . . and beyond

Kinjal Dave can trace her interest in space and aerospace back to when she was at primary school in India.

ADRIAN POPE

Kinjal Dave, BAE Systems

Analytics consultant Kinjal Dave was just six years old at the time of the 2003 Space Shuttle Columbia disaster.

"It killed all seven astronauts aboard, including the first India-born woman astronaut to go into space, Kalpana Chawla," describes Dave. "I remember it was a huge shock for me but from that day onwards, I knew I wanted to become an astronaut or a fighter pilot when I grew up."

By the time Dave was applying for university, she had worked out how she could join the space and aerospace industry.

"Health issues while I was growing up meant I'd been rejected by the RAF as a cadet," she explains. "But during my A-levels I became really interested in the materials science aspect of space and aerospace. It's a perfect marriage between two of the subjects I was studying – chemistry and physics."

She studied aeronautical and astronautical engineering at Queen Mary University of London. "It was a great course that was supported by industry, with visits to places like Tilbury Power Station and Airbus," Dave remembers.

"I spent a lot of my time at university looking at propulsion and space debris, as well as alternative sources to power spacecrafts," she continues. "And that's what got me interested in nuclear power."

Following her graduation, Dave opted to do a one-year masters in nuclear energy at the University of Cambridge.

"Nuclear power doesn't get as much attention as it should, mainly because of people's fears over nuclear waste, weapons and war," she explains. "But the Cambridge syllabus focused on the safety aspect of nuclear physics and it was matched very closely to what was going on in industry. It was a real eye-opener for me to see how many scientific advancements have come from nuclear power."

Dave made job applications to all the major defence and aerospace companies during her masters course, but also considered working as a consultant too. "BAE Systems was top of my list because its business included nuclear submarines and lots of work in the space and air sectors," she remembers.

"And I was a bit old-fashioned and opinionated about consultancy – in that nobody gives any importance to a 22 year-old consultant," continues Dave. "You need to have some experience of different industries, department, functions, cultures and places in order to be credible."

BAE Systems offered Dave a role as a technical consultant at its Digital Intelligence business in Farnborough. "The first few months were a very, very steep learning curve, as I took on the role of project manager for eight different projects," she explains. "It was a real eye-opener but it was a very collaborative environment with plenty of people to reach out to for help."

After eight months, Dave moved to BAE Systems in Chelmsford. "It's their labs site and I did some really hands-on engineering work and material science, looking at directed energy sources," she explains. "I also worked on indoor navigation and systems engineering for space."

Over the past five years, Dave has worked with a wide range of clients, including central government, diplomats, international commercial customers and the Ministry of Defence.

She has built up experience of change management, financial modelling, bidding for contracts, practical engineering and research & development, and continues to draw heavily on both her university degrees. "Although it's owned by BAE Systems, I'm proud that I actually have my own patent, for a solution I developed for space debris," Dave enthuses.

"My current job title is analytics consultant, which means my day job is looking at data and working with defence customers and clients," she continues. "But at the heart of it, it's the engineering and science that I really enjoy."

At the forefront of children's social work

The launch of a brand new graduate programme eight years ago proved to be very timely for Brydee Lynch, when she was looking into her options for after university.

She was studying for the criminology and law degree at Leeds Beckett University. "I thought I wanted to work in youth justice or perhaps for the police," remembers Lynch. "But I quickly realised that if I was going to get into youth justice, I would need to get experience of social work."

Lynch was due to leave university in 2014, the first year that the Frontline programme started recruiting graduates to become children's social workers, beginning with an initial cohort of a hundred university-leavers, many of whom hadn't previously considered a career in social work.

"Both my parents were actually social workers and I'd been really against just going down the same route as them. But it was my Mum who saw details of the new programme and recommended it to me," explains Lynch. "I applied and they offered me a place in their very first intake."

Her training on the Frontline programme began with a five-week intensive summer institute before she joined a local authority in Manchester.

"I was one of four Frontline participants who were working together in the same team, under the guidance of a consultant social worker," Lynch says.

"She was the allocated social worker for the families that we were working with, and we were helping her. It was quite daunting but exciting to be involved in real child protection cases straightaway. It was a great way to learn and develop and was good to be able to see how a qualified social worker reached their decisions about difficult situations."

Her work included a number of complex and high-risk cases. "I was

Brydee Lynch, former Frontline participant and consultant social worker

involved in several cases that went to court, where children went on to be adopted," explains Lynch. "But it was all with the support of the consultant social worker and with the benefit of her knowledge and experience."

Although Frontline is a two-year programme, participants become qualified social workers after just twelve months.

"You do various assignments, practical work, and university study days during that first year, as you work towards the first 120 credits of your master's degree in social work," explains Lynch.

"Once you are registered with the professional body, then you move into the main teams within the local authority. You're a qualified social

worker with your own caseload from that point on."

She continued to work in the team that she'd joined in her first year. "Because I was at an inner-city authority, there was a great deal of deprivation and poverty and we'd see lots of issues relating to that," Lynch remembers.

"I got to work with a really diverse range of families that helped me understand different religions, backgrounds and cultures and how that affects parenting."

She admits it was intense at times and emotionally challenging. "But Frontline puts a great deal of focus on resilience and how we protect and support ourselves," she says.

After two years in Manchester, Lynch transferred to the child protection team at a smaller local authority in neighbouring Trafford, and later went on to become a consultant social worker herself, mentoring and training the next generation of participants on the Frontline programme.

"I was over the moon they asked me and I really enjoyed supporting three cohorts of new participants through the programme," she says. "It was a steep learning curve for me too, stepping into that role, but it was great to be able to use my experience and reconnect with the theories and models that Frontline uses to deliver its training and development."

Lynch went on to join the local authority in Cheshire West and Chester in September 2020 as a senior practice lead. "But after more than six years in child protection, I've recently moved to a new role within the fostering service," she explains.

"It's a great opportunity for me and means I can continue to broaden my skills and learn about a different area of social work."

Do extraordinary things. Every day.

Join a global business that powers industry, fuels innovation, and connects us all, with endless opportunities to do extraordinary things.

Discover a career that makes a real difference to the world.

BT Group

This is the work where you'll build the skills that help change lives

This is social work

Interested in a career that matters?
Apply to the Frontline programme today.

Front|ine

On the fast track to the heart of Government

After studying a physics degree at university, Rian Johnson is now an up-and-coming civil servant working on the nation's energy policy.

Rian Johnson grew up in the Liverpool area and was keen to study at a local university.

"With having a disability, I wanted to continue living at home, so I chose to do physics at the University of Liverpool," he explains. "I really enjoy the subject because I love how complicated it can be but also how practical it is and it really helps you understand how things around you work."

When he started his degree, Johnson didn't have a specific career in mind for after university.

"I knew that there were lots of different things I could do after studying physics, whether it was banking or accountancy or perhaps a career in academia," he remembers. "But it was seeing that the Civil Service was number one in *The Times Top 100 Graduate Employers* that got me interested."

Johnson applied for a place on the Civil Service Science & Engineering Fast Stream programme at the beginning of his final year.

"I thought the chances of getting in were pretty low because of all the competition but I knew the application and selection process would be good experience," he recalls. The process included online psychometric tests, a scenario-based situational judgement test, and then a recorded video interview.

"These are tough because you think of so much to say but you've only got thirty seconds to give each answer," continues Johnson. "And you've got to be convincing for the person watching the interview."

The next stage was a half day assessment centre. "It included leadership and team exercises – and tested your decision-making and how you work together with other candidates," he explains. "It's

definitely worth getting some practice for these types of exercises beforehand because they are so different to what you'll have done during your degree. I'd failed a similar assessment centre for one of the accounting firms a couple of weeks earlier because I'd been so nervous about them."

This time, though, Johnson was successful and reached the final round of the Fast Stream selection, which tests applicants on their technical knowledge and abilities.

"I was given resources like news reports, scientific reports and industry documents – and told that I needed to brief the Minister in an hour!" remembers Johnson.

"There's lots of information to read, condense and explain in a way that someone without a scientific background could understand. And then you give a five-minute presentation to a selection panel and interviews about your scientific experience."

Johnson learned at Easter that he'd been awarded a place on the programme and started work on his first Fast Stream placement in October 2021.

"I joined the Department of Business, Energy and Industrial Strategy (BEIS), working mainly from home because of the continuing pandemic," he explains. "The Fast Stream has been very welcoming and as a disabled applicant, asked me very early on about making workplace adjustments for me. It showed me that I was in good hands and that it

Rian Johnson, Civil Service Fast Stream

would be a supportive environment."

His first posting has been in the established renewables policy team at BEIS, working on solar and onshore wind power.

"It's an incredibly busy area, especially in the run-up to last year's COP26 UN Climate Change Conference," he says. "I've been doing research, working with scientists, giving presentations and briefings to ministers and senior civil servants about renewable sources of energy."

"I've had an amazing year. I was able to contribute to the Government's 'net zero' policies, and more recently on the British energy security strategy, to safeguard our energy supplies following the Ukraine crisis," enthuses Johnson.

"And I even got to meet Sir Patrick Vallance, the Government's Chief Scientific Adviser at one of the regular breakfast meetings he holds for science and engineering Fast Streamers," he continues.

"I'm proud to have done so many things that I never imagined myself doing twelve months ago."

Suzannah Clarke, KPMG

ACCOUNTING & PROFESSIONAL SERVICES

Accounting for career success

It wasn't during her accounting and finance degree at the University of Exeter or at the university's careers fair that Suzannah Clarke first discovered KPMG, the accounting & professional services firm.

When I was at Exeter, KPMG sponsored many of the university sports teams and student societies, so they had a really good presence on-campus," remembers Clarke.

She applied to the firm in her final year and was invited to an assessment centre. "I had a great experience," she says. "It was a day in London and gave me such a good introduction to the culture at the firm and what it does. It was so well run and made the firm seem very enticing!"

Clarke was offered a graduate trainee position at the firm and joined one of its corporate audit teams in London after graduating from Exeter in the summer of 2017.

"Working in audit means reviewing the financial statements from companies or businesses, checking the wording and numbers, to ensure that everything they are presenting is correct," she explains. "It has to be in accordance with financial regulations

and comply with what the regulators require them to disclose."

Clarke found herself working on audit engagements almost immediately. "My first day of work was in the office on a Monday and then on the Tuesday we flew to Amsterdam," she enthuses. "I was very lucky to get that opportunity so quickly and spent two weeks there working on my first audit."

For the first three years, trainees combine working at the firm with studying for their professional accountancy exams.

"You're juggling multiple priorities but there's college days and planned study leave to help you revise for the exams," explains Clarke. "And you have real world examples from your day-to-day work that can be really helpful, because you've seen the theory working in practice."

During her training, Clarke worked out of the office for much of the time. "I spent about 80% of

my time working at the offices of the companies we were auditing," she remembers. "I had one big engagement in central London and they had a huge room which meant our whole team could work together there, which was great. It's the best way to learn."

Clarke qualified as a chartered accountant in October 2020 and was promoted to assistant manager. "It opens up a lot more opportunities at that stage," she explains. "You can start working directly with senior managers and partners and develop new skills like coaching or mentoring, to help train and develop new joiners."

It also brings more responsibility too. "Within a year of qualifying, I had the chance to present to a client's Chief Finance Officer in a senior management meeting, which was something I didn't believe I'd be doing so soon," she says.

After just eighteen months as an assistant manager, Clarke was promoted again, this time to manager. "Progression at the firm is based on your performance and how well you're working on the jobs you're doing," she continues.

"The more senior you get, the more we understand the organisations we're working with. I really enjoy the high-level business conversations that we have and the incredible insight you get from that."

And as a manager, Clarke now runs her own audit team. "I'm managing a team of seven or eight but when we get to the firm's busiest times of the year we'll have even more," she explains.

Five years into her career, Clarke is as passionate as ever about working in audit. "When you complete an audit, there's such a sense of achievement about the work we've done," she enthuses.

"On the day that the partner leading the audit signs the accounts, you get a huge feeling of 'wow, look what we've done as a team', it's incredibly satisfying."

Expect collaboration _

One firm, one team

Application windows 2022/23

Programme	Open	Close
Workshop	10 October	15 November
Summer vacation scheme	10 October	7 December
London – Asia training contract	10 October	5 January
Winter training contract	10 October	5 January
Spring scheme	10 October	16 February
Summer training contract	1 June	7 July

At Freshfields you will be building the future, laying the foundations of your career with high-profile, precedent-setting international work.
If you're creative, and curious about different ways of doing things and you like to work in teams, Freshfields is the place for you.

- Eight-seat training contract
- Globally recognised clients
- A focus on people, diversity and inclusion
- International secondment opportunities
- Innovation and legal technology
- Comprehensive mental health and wellbeing support
- Hybrid Working

f @FreshfieldsGraduates

in Freshfields Bruckhaus Deringer

𝕏 @FreshfieldsGrad

◉ @FreshfieldsGrads

Apply now
freshfields.com/ukgraduates

 Freshfields

THE ✦ TIMES
THE SUNDAY TIMES
Know your times

Six months free access to Perlego

Open doors with a student subscription for just £1.99 a month.

Get the most out of university with a digital subscription to The Times and The Sunday Times. The first month is free, plus you get six months complimentary access to Perlego's online library of academic resources and tools.

Subscribe today at thetimes.co.uk/student

THE TIMES
TOP 100
GRADUATE EMPLOYERS

EMPLOYER	RANK	Accountancy	Consulting	Engineering	Finance	General Management	Human Resources	Investment Banking	Law	Logistics	Marketing	Media	Property	Purchasing	Research & Development	Retail	Sales	Technology	Other	VACANCIES	Insight Courses	Degree Placements	Summer Internships	PAGE
AIRBUS	75			●	●		●				●			●	●			●		300+		●		74
ALDI	9				●									●						100		●		76
AMAZON	10			●	●	●	●		●									●		1300+		●	●	78
AON	82		●		●			●										●		200		●	●	80
ARCADIS	77		●	●														●		200		●	●	82
ASTRAZENECA	22		●	●				●						●				●		40+		●	●	84
BAE SYSTEMS	25	●	●	●	●	●	●		●							●	●	●		600+	●	●	●	86
BAKER MCKENZIE	74						●											●		40	●		●	88
BANK OF AMERICA	61	●		●		●												●		No fixed quota	●	●	●	90
BBC	7		●	●	●		●		●		●	●		●				●		200+			●	92
BCG	30		●																	No fixed quota			●	94
BDO	51	●																		700		●	●	96
BLACKROCK	49			●	●			●								●	●			100+	●	●	●	98
BLOOMBERG	42		●	●												●	●	●	●	350+	●		●	100
BP	40		●	●	●			●			●		●	●		●	●			100+				102
BT	47		●	●	●				●					●			●			250		●	●	104
CIVIL SERVICE	1		●	●	●	●				●	●		●				●			No fixed quota			●	106
CLYDE & CO	91						●													75+				108
CMS	60						●													95				110
CREDIT SUISSE	83			●		●												●		200+	●	●	●	112
DELOITTE	4	●	●		●		●		●			●						●		1,000+	●	●	●	114
DEUTSCHE BANK	57			●		●												●		100+	●	●	●	116
DYSON	71		●	●	●		●			●				●				●		300		●	●	118
ENTERPRISE	99				●											●	●			800+		●	●	120
EVERSHEDS SUTHERLAND	92					●														40			●	122
EY	6	●	●		●													●		1,000+	●	●	●	124
FRESHFIELDS	88						●													90+	●		●	126
FRONTLINE	43																		●	480			●	128
GCHQ	79		●		●									●				●		200+	●	●	●	130
GOLDMAN SACHS	11	●		●	●		●	●	●					●		●	●	●		400	●	●	●	132
GOOGLE	5		●	●	●		●			●					●	●	●			No fixed quota			●	134
GRANT THORNTON	96	●	●	●																350-400		●	●	136
GSK	13		●	●	●		●		●	●	●		●	●	●	●			35+		●	●	138
HALEON	–		●	●		●			●	●			●	●		●	●			20+	●	●	●	140
HSBC	16		●	●	●		●										●			600+	●	●	●	142
J.P. MORGAN	12	●	●		●	●	●	●						●		●				500	●	●	●	144
KPMG	8	●	●		●	●		●									●			1,000+	●	●	●	146
KUBRICK	89		●	●													●			900+				148

We only recruit one type of person

FEMALEBLACKMALE ASIANSCHOOLLEAVER GRADUATEDISABLED GAYLOWINCOMEWHITE TRANSGENDERCAREER CHANGERNEURODIVERSE BRITISHCITIZEN

At the UK intelligence services, we believe that with the right mix of minds, anything is possible. So, we don't recruit a particular 'type' of person. We need people who can bring a rich mix of skills, experiences and backgrounds to help us fight the threats we face.

Although each service has a slightly different remit, we all work towards one aim: protecting the UK and its people, at home and overseas. With a truly diverse workforce, we can keep the country safe.

MI5 protects the UK from threats to national security, such as terrorism and espionage. How? By gathering intelligence and working closely with our partners, we detect such threats and work out ways to stop them. Find us at: **www.mi5.gov.uk/careers**

MI6 works with the UK's foreign partners to support global stability by combating international terrorism and the spread of weapons. So, we work secretly around the world and in the UK, to stay ahead of our adversaries. Discover more: **www.sis.gov.uk**

GCHQ uses the ingenuity of our people and cutting-edge technology to protect the UK in the real world and online. That means we work with a wide range of partners to identify, analyse and stop cyber attacks, terrorism and serious crime. **www.gchq-careers.co.uk**

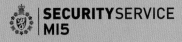  

AIRBUS

Airbus is always at the forefront of innovating new technologies, with a pioneering spirit that has redefined the aerospace industry. Its products bring people closer together, helping them unite and progress. Airbus strives to continually push the boundaries on what is possible to safeguard the world for future generations.

Every year Airbus looks for university graduates from around the world to join them. Airbus needs people with the aspiration, enthusiasm and the talent to help them move forward and to change the world – to deliver their vision to pioneer sustainable aerospace for a safe and united world. This year they have an exciting opportunity to welcome more graduates into the family, with the Airbus Global Graduate Programme (AGGP).

This programme aims to help graduates take flight with their career, joining on a development pathway that will assist their growth into specifically skilled positions. Graduates will be part of a global community that come together once a year for a conference where they meet peers, hear from leaders and learn from the best.

Over the course of the programme, they can also gain experience through a series of rotational placements. The placements are tailored to suit each graduate's needs, as well as those of the business, encouraging individuals to take control of their own career.

Airbus has opportunities across all the divisions within a multitude of functions – Engineering, Finance, Marketing, Customer Support, Procurement, Cyber to name but a few!

What's more, working alongside passionate and determined people, Airbus graduates will help to accomplish the extraordinary – on the ground, in the sky, and in space.

GRADUATE VACANCIES IN 2023
ENGINEERING
FINANCE
HUMAN RESOURCES
MARKETING
PURCHASING
RESEARCH & DEVELOPMENT
TECHNOLOGY

NUMBER OF VACANCIES
300+ graduate jobs

LOCATIONS OF VACANCIES

Vacancies also available in Europe, Asia and the USA.

STARTING SALARY FOR 2023
£Competitive

WORK EXPERIENCE
DEGREE
PLACEMENTS

UNIVERSITY PROMOTIONS DURING 2022-2023
ASTON, BATH, BRISTOL, EDINBURGH, EXETER, GLASGOW, IMPERIAL COLLEGE LONDON, LANCASTER, LIVERPOOL, LOUGHBOROUGH, MANCHESTER, SHEFFIELD, SOUTHAMPTON, STRATHCLYDE, SWANSEA
Please check with your university careers service for full details of Airbus' local promotions and events.

MINIMUM ENTRY REQUIREMENTS
Varies by function
Relevant degree required for some roles.

APPLICATION DEADLINE
6th November 2022

FURTHER INFORMATION
www.Top100GraduateEmployers.com
Register now for the latest news, local promotions, work experience and graduate vacancies at Airbus.

READY TO
MAKE A
DIFFERENCE?

Join the Airbus Global Graduate Programme.

We need people with the aspiration, enthusiasm and the talent to help us move forward and to change the world, delivering on our vision to pioneer sustainable aerospace for a safe and united world.

Start your development journey with the Airbus Global Graduate Programme, applications open 19 September 2022.

airbus.com/careers in linkedin.com/company/airbusgroup f facebook.com/airbuscareers 🐦 @AirbusCareers 📷 @WeAreAirbus

AIRBUS

Aldi arrived in the UK back in 1990 and is now one of the fastest growing supermarkets. Just like their business growth, Graduate Area Managers will progress at pace. Over 12 months, exceptional training and mentorship will steer graduates on their way to managing their own £multi-million business.

There are many reasons to join the Graduate Area Manager programme: the responsibility, the exposure, the support…and yes, the salary and the car. But top of the list should be the opportunity to get involved, give more – and get even more back! Within the first 12 months, graduates will become responsible for a portfolio of stores, experiencing mind-stretching retail challenges that will sharpen their commercial edge and enable them to make business critical decisions throughout their career journey. It's the perfect introduction to Aldi and a superb foundation for future success.

Depending on business needs, graduates with the willingness and drive to be flexible in both their areas of responsibility and location may get the chance to take on a project role within one of Aldi's Regions, National departments, or even an International Secondment. Beyond that, high-performing Area Managers could even move into a Director role. Don't shop around – with enthusiasm and ambition, this is the chance to become a future leader at Aldi.

The key to Aldi's success is the people – without them, it wouldn't be possible. It's a business with integrity – fair to partners and suppliers, and everything it does is for the benefit of customers, colleagues and the community – whether that's through lowering the cost of groceries for millions of customers, supporting British suppliers or taking steps to create an inclusive workplace for everyone in Team Aldi.

Simply put, Aldi means more.

GRADUATE VACANCIES IN 2023

GENERAL MANAGEMENT

RETAIL

NUMBER OF VACANCIES
100 graduate jobs

LOCATIONS OF VACANCIES

STARTING SALARY FOR 2023
£44,000

WORK EXPERIENCE
DEGREE PLACEMENTS

UNIVERSITY PROMOTIONS DURING 2022-2023
ABERYSTWYTH, BATH, BIRMINGHAM, CAMBRIDGE, CARDIFF, EDINBURGH, GLASGOW, HULL, KING'S COLLEGE LONDON, LANCASTER, LEEDS, LIVERPOOL, LOUGHBOROUGH, MANCHESTER, NEWCASTLE, NORTHUMBRIA, NOTTINGHAM, OXFORD, READING, SHEFFIELD, SOUTHAMPTON, ST ANDREWS, STRATHCLYDE, SURREY, SUSSEX, SWANSEA, UEA, UNIVERSITY COLLEGE LONDON, YORK
Please check with your university careers service for full details of Aldi's local promotions and events.

MINIMUM ENTRY REQUIREMENTS
2.1 Degree, 96 UCAS points

APPLICATION DEADLINE
Year-round recruitment
Early application is advised

FURTHER INFORMATION
www.Top100GraduateEmployers.com
Register now for the latest news, local promotions, work experience and graduate vacancies at Aldi.

Amazon's mission is to be Earth's most customer-centric company. This is what unites Amazonians across teams and geographies as they are all striving to delight customers and make their lives easier, one innovative product, service, and idea at a time.

Every year, Amazon offers hundreds of graduates the opportunity to design their path to a successful career. Starting from Day 1, graduates are given a leadership position with significant responsibilities. Amazon believes in hiring and developing the best; their graduates are given numerous opportunities to acquire technical skills that will enable them to take on future opportunities within the company. By working on behalf of its customers, Amazon is building the future - one innovative product, service and idea at a time.

Amazon encourages graduates to have a self-starter mentality when it comes to learning, and they supplement this with hands-on training to enable their people to progress and succeed.

There are opportunities across a broad spectrum of teams, and many graduates join the organisation as Area Managers, who lead and develop teams. Amazon hires the brightest minds and offers them the platform to think around corners and innovate on behalf of their customers.

Amazon is a company of builders who bring varying backgrounds, ideas, and points of view to inventing on behalf of their customers. Amazon's diverse perspectives come from many sources including gender, race, age, national origin, sexual orientation, culture, education, and professional and life experience.

Amazon is committed to diversity and inclusion and always look for ways to scale their impact as they grow.

GRADUATE VACANCIES IN 2023

ENGINEERING
FINANCE
GENERAL MANAGEMENT
HUMAN RESOURCES
LOGISTICS
TECHNOLOGY

NUMBER OF VACANCIES
1300+ graduate jobs

LOCATIONS OF VACANCIES

STARTING SALARY FOR 2023
£Competitive
Plus relocation, sign-on and shares bonuses.

WORK EXPERIENCE
DEGREE PLACEMENTS | SUMMER INTERNSHIPS

UNIVERSITY PROMOTIONS DURING 2022-2023
ASTON, BATH, BIRMINGHAM, BRISTOL, CAMBRIDGE, CARDIFF, DURHAM, EDINBURGH, EXETER, GLASGOW, IMPERIAL COLLEGE LONDON, KING'S COLLEGE LONDON, LANCASTER, LEEDS, LIVERPOOL, LOUGHBOROUGH, MANCHESTER, NEWCASTLE, NOTTINGHAM, OXFORD, READING, SHEFFIELD, SOUTHAMPTON, ST ANDREWS, STRATHCLYDE, UNIVERSITY COLLEGE LONDON, WARWICK, YORK
Please check with your university careers service for full details of Amazon's local promotions and events.

MINIMUM ENTRY REQUIREMENTS
Any degree accepted

APPLICATION DEADLINE
Year-round recruitment
Early application is advised.

FURTHER INFORMATION
www.Top100GraduateEmployers.com
*Register now for the latest news, local promotions, work experience and graduate vacancies at **Amazon**.*

We are hiring
1300+ Graduates

Come build the
future with us

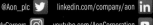

AON

Aon delivers innovative solutions that address the un-met needs stemming from today's rapidly changing, increasingly complex and interconnected challenges. Regardless of industry, size or geography, Aon deliver solutions to help clients stay better informed, better advised and able to make better decisions.

A United Aon: Aon believes that businesses thrive when the communities they serve and the people they employ also flourish. Aon's values are the foundation of what they do.

They are: Committed as one firm to their purpose. United through trust as one inclusive, diverse team. Passionate about making their colleagues and clients successful.

Depending on the area they join, Aon's graduates will be using their analytical mindset, commercial awareness, and strong communication skills to help clients address the key questions that affect their businesses. What will be the impact of rising life expectancy? How would the collapse of the Eurozone affect the world economy? Aon's business is to provide the answers.

Graduates join Aon across a range of consulting and broking roles within business areas including Actuarial, Investment, Insurance and Reinsurance, Insurance Strategy, Employee Benefits, Reward and Remuneration, Talent and Employee Engagement and Cybersecurity.

Aon's Launch development programme is designed to support and develop the future stars of the business by helping graduates to build their business knowledge and learn how to grow effective relationships with clients and colleagues. In addition to technical training, colleagues are fully supported to study for relevant professional qualifications to enable them to have a greater impact on Aon's clients and progress within their chosen career path.

GRADUATE VACANCIES IN 2023

CONSULTING

FINANCE

INVESTMENT BANKING

TECHNOLOGY

NUMBER OF VACANCIES
200 graduate jobs

LOCATIONS OF VACANCIES

Vacancies also available worldwide.

STARTING SALARY FOR 2023
£Competitive

WORK EXPERIENCE

| DEGREE PLACEMENTS | SUMMER INTERNSHIPS |

UNIVERSITY PROMOTIONS DURING 2022-2023
ASTON, BATH, BIRMINGHAM, BRISTOL, CITY, DURHAM, EDINBURGH, ESSEX, EXETER, HERIOT-WATT, IMPERIAL COLLEGE LONDON, KENT, LANCASTER, LEEDS, LEICESTER, MANCHESTER, NOTTINGHAM, ROYAL HOLLOWAY, SOUTHAMPTON, SURREY, UNIVERSITY COLLEGE LONDON, WARWICK
Please check with your university careers service for full details of Aon's local promotions and events.

MINIMUM ENTRY REQUIREMENTS
2.1 Degree

APPLICATION DEADLINE
Varies by function

FURTHER INFORMATION
www.Top100GraduateEmployers.com
Register now for the latest news, local promotions, work experience and graduate vacancies at Aon.

AON

Make Better Decisions

At Aon, we believe businesses succeed when the communities they serve — and the people they employ — flourish. Our purpose is to shape decisions for the better — to protect and enrich the lives of people around the world.

Let us help you make a better career decision!

We have consulting & broking opportunities for graduates, undergraduates and apprentices available in Actuarial, Investment, Insurance & Reinsurance, Insurance Strategy, Employee Benefits, Reward & Renumeration and Talent & Employee Engagement.

Visit our website to find out more:
www.aonearlycareers.co.uk

#Aonearlycareers

Sarika Pabari, Graduate

earlycareers@arcadis.com ✉

@ArcadisUK 🐦   ArcadisGlobal f

@ArcadisGlobal 📷   linkedin.com/company/arcadis in

ARCADIS

Arcadis is the world's leading company delivering sustainable design, engineering and consultancy solutions for natural and built assets. Right now, more than 29,000 Arcadians across 70 countries are working to address the world's challenges, such as climate change, urbanisation, digitalisation and poverty.

Arcadis' story began back in 1888 in the Netherlands, where they developed unusable land into places for people to live and establish communities.

Nowadays, they focus on creating better housing, revolutionising transport systems and finding new solutions to complex environmental challenges. Arcadis embeds sustainability across everything they do to deliver solutions that are resilient, effective and within planetary boundaries.

The future of Arcadis is being shaped by the mindset of its people. That is why the organisation constantly seeks fresh thinkers who are innovators that challenge the status quo and are problem solvers for the planet.

The Arcadis Graduate GROW Scheme is a three-year accelerated learning programme focused on shaping Arcadians to become the leaders of the future. They offer opportunities in Engineering, Consulting, Project Management and Environmental disciplines. Arcadis' graduates are supported from day one with structured training, mentoring, as well as support for gaining industry accreditations.

Arcadis' 'People First' culture propelled the company to become one of the Best Big Companies to Work For in the UK in 2021, and Glassdoor's Best Places to Work for in 2022. They are committed to providing an innovative and healthy work environment for Arcadians where flexibility, sustainability, DE&I and charitable works sit at the core.

At Arcadis, graduates can build a world they want to be part of.

GRADUATE VACANCIES IN 2023
CONSULTING
ENGINEERING

NUMBER OF VACANCIES
200 graduate jobs

LOCATIONS OF VACANCIES

STARTING SALARY FOR 2023
£25,250-£34,000

WORK EXPERIENCE
DEGREE PLACEMENTS | SUMMER INTERNSHIPS

UNIVERSITY PROMOTIONS DURING 2022-2023
BATH, BIRMINGHAM, BRISTOL, CARDIFF, EXETER, GLASGOW, LANCASTER, LEEDS, LIVERPOOL, LOUGHBOROUGH, MANCHESTER, READING, SOUTHAMPTON, UNIVERSITY COLLEGE LONDON
Please check with your university careers service for full details of Arcadis' local promotions and events.

MINIMUM ENTRY REQUIREMENTS
Varies by function
Relevant degree required for some roles.

APPLICATION DEADLINE
Varies by function

FURTHER INFORMATION
www.Top100GraduateEmployers.com
*Register now for the latest news, local promotions, work experience and graduate vacancies at **Arcadis**.*

Become a
problem solver
for the planet

We're constantly seeking innovative
thinkers who challenge everything,
to build a world they want to be part of.

Join us and improve quality of life.

AstraZeneca

AstraZeneca is a global, science-led, patient-focused biopharmaceutical company employing 70,000 people worldwide. They focus on the discovery, development and commercialisation of prescription medicines for some of the world's most serious disease.

AstraZeneca's graduate programmes offer huge variety when it comes to graduate learning and potential for growth.

Graduates are empowered to jump in, take the initiative and be part of meaningful project teams, and make an impact by delivering real value to patients and business.

Their programmes place an emphasis on personal and professional development, and invest in each graduate's unique interests and potential.

Working in a fast-paced, yet deeply supportive and collaborative environment, graduates are encouraged to take responsibility and put their knowledge into practice, whilst being supported by inspiring peers.

Astraeneca's graduates work hard, building a rich and supportive network that will last a lifetime. Graduates have significant opportunities to build bonds with their international peers, developing connections and growing their network with experts and leaders across the business.

Programmes bring diverse talent from all over the world together to gain an international perspective and combine strengths and knowledge to multiply impact.

AstraZeneca is proud of their award-winning, progressive working practices. They welcome diverse thinking, curiosity, collaboration and the courage to go further, together. To find out more about becoming a part of their team, visit the early talent pages of their global careers site.

GRADUATE VACANCIES IN 2023
ENGINEERING
FINANCE
LOGISTICS
RESEARCH & DEVELOPMENT
TECHNOLOGY

NUMBER OF VACANCIES
40+ graduate jobs

LOCATIONS OF VACANCIES

Vacancies also available across Europe, the USA and Asia.

STARTING SALARY FOR 2023
£31,000+
Plus competitive benefits and bonuses.

WORK EXPERIENCE
DEGREE PLACEMENTS   SUMMER INTERNSHIPS

UNIVERSITY PROMOTIONS DURING 2022-2023
BIRMINGHAM, CAMBRIDGE, EDINBURGH, KING'S COLLEGE LONDON, MANCHESTER, NOTTINGHAM, QUEEN MARY LONDON, STRATHCLYDE, UNIVERSITY COLLEGE LONDON, WARWICK
Please check with your university careers service for full details of AstraZenaca's local promotions and events.

MINIMUM ENTRY REQUIREMENTS
Varies by function
Relevant degree required for some roles.

APPLICATION DEADLINE
Varies by function
Please see website for full details.

FURTHER INFORMATION
www.Top100GraduateEmployers.com
Register now for the latest news, local promotions, work experience and graduate vacancies at AstraZenaca.

AstraZeneca

Make an impact and kickstart your career

We have exciting and rewarding Graduate Programmes in:

- Biometrics & Clinical Data
- BioPharmaceutical Development
- Data Sciences & Artificial Intelligence
- IT/Technology Leadership
- Operations & Supply Chain
- Patient Safety
- Pharmaceutical Technology & Development
- Precision Medicines
- Research & Development

Starting salary for 2023

£31,000+

Plus bonus, benefits
& relocation (if applicable)

*AstraZeneca is an equal
opportunity employer*

For more information and to apply, please visit:
careers.astrazeneca.com/early-talent

@LifeatBAESystems linkedin.com/company/bae-systems

BAE Systems helps to protect people and national security, critical infrastructure and vital information. It's a culture that values diversity, rewards integrity and merit, and is a place where everyone has the opportunity to fulfil their potential, no matter what their background.

With a workforce of 90,500 people in more than 40 countries, BAE Systems is committed to nurturing talent and striving for excellence – empowering their people to drive innovation, make the right decisions, and solve complex challenges. Be part of a collaborative culture creating the next generation of security products and services, BAE Systems is a place graduates and undergraduates can start and grow their career with confidence.

Wherever their career interests lie – from project management, technology and engineering, to manufacturing, consulting and finance, or wider business disciplines – at BAE Systems, graduates have the chance to make a real impact, whichever team they join.

With opportunities nationwide, joining a BAE Systems programme means working alongside the brightest minds and learning through valuable hands-on experience and formal training – developing a career, from day one. They'll be able to pace their own programme length from 18-30 months, to match their career aspirations and personal learning journey, and on completion graduates could even find themselves on BAE Systems' Future Talent Programme.

New graduates will be part of a culture that's committed to working to high ethical and environmental standards, in an inclusive work environment. Making a positive contribution to the countries and communities in which they operate. Embrace the opportunity – apply now.

GRADUATE VACANCIES IN 2023

ACCOUNTANCY
CONSULTING
ENGINEERING
FINANCE
GENERAL MANAGEMENT
HUMAN RESOURCES
MARKETING
SALES
TECHNOLOGY

NUMBER OF VACANCIES
600+ graduate jobs

LOCATIONS OF VACANCIES

STARTING SALARY FOR 2023
£30,000

WORK EXPERIENCE

INSIGHT COURSES	DEGREE PLACEMENTS	SUMMER INTERNSHIPS

UNIVERSITY PROMOTIONS DURING 2022-2023
ASTON, BATH, BIRMINGHAM, BRISTOL, BRUNEL, EDINBURGH, GLASGOW, IMPERIAL COLLEGE LONDON, KENT, LANCASTER, LEICESTER, LIVERPOOL, LOUGHBOROUGH, MANCHESTER, NEWCASTLE, NORTHUMBRIA, QUEEN MARY LONDON, SHEFFIELD, SOUTHAMPTON, STRATHCLYDE, SURREY, UNIVERSITY COLLEGE LONDON, WARWICK
Please check with your university careers service for full details of BAE Systems' local promotions and events.

MINIMUM ENTRY REQUIREMENTS
Varies by function
Relevant degree required for some roles.

APPLICATION DEADLINE
Varies by function

FURTHER INFORMATION
www.Top100GraduateEmployers.com
Register now for the latest news, local promotions, work experience and graduate vacancies at BAE Systems.

With over 13,000 people in 77 offices around the world, Baker McKenzie prides itself on being a truly innovative and diverse law firm. In the current climate, that's never been more important. It also enables them to go above and beyond for their clients, collaborating across borders, markets and industries.

Working at Baker McKenzie means being challenged. It means being supported, nurtured and valued. Yes, it's a big firm but not so big that they don't realise the importance of bright new talent. In fact, the Firm goes to extraordinary lengths to bring out the best in its graduates, giving them access to a broad range of legal work.

As Trainee Solicitors, graduates at Baker McKenzie liaise directly with clients on high-profile cases. They contribute to important meetings and prepare a broad range of legal documents. They also get the chance to apply for a six-month secondment at one of the Firm's international offices. Past trainees have spent time in Brussels, Dubai, New York, San Francisco, Singapore, Sydney and Tokyo. Trainees can also apply for client secondments and learn whilst partnering with some of the world's biggest brands.

When it comes to inclusion and diversity, the Firm invests in a number of employee affinity networks committed to cultural diversity, the LGBT+ community, mental health and wellbeing, social mobility and more. In terms of culture, Baker McKenzie promotes a positive, high-performing working environment where creativity is encouraged, and different points of view are always appreciated. The Firm also has many different clubs, societies and social events to allow employees to get to know each other away from their desks.

To learn more about life as a Trainee Solicitor at Baker McKenzie and to formally apply, visit Baker McKenzie's graduate recruitment website online.

GRADUATE VACANCIES IN 2023
LAW

NUMBER OF VACANCIES
40 graduate jobs
For training contracts starting in 2025.

LOCATIONS OF VACANCIES

STARTING SALARY FOR 2023
£50,000

WORK EXPERIENCE
INSIGHT COURSES | SUMMER INTERNSHIPS

UNIVERSITY PROMOTIONS DURING 2022-2023
ABERDEEN, BATH, BELFAST, BIRMINGHAM, BRISTOL, CAMBRIDGE, CARDIFF, DURHAM, EDINBURGH, ESSEX, EXETER, GLASGOW, KING'S COLLEGE LONDON, KENT, LANCASTER, LEEDS, LEICESTER, LIVERPOOL, LONDON SCHOOL OF ECONOMICS, MANCHESTER, NEWCASTLE, NOTTINGHAM, OXFORD, QUEEN MARY LONDON, SOUTHAMPTON, ST ANDREWS, SWANSEA, UEA, UNIVERSITY COLLEGE LONDON, WARWICK, YORK
Please check with your university careers service for full details of Baker McKenzie's local promotions and events.

MINIMUM ENTRY REQUIREMENTS
2.1 Degree

APPLICATION DEADLINE
Year-round recruitment
Early application is advised

FURTHER INFORMATION
www.Top100GraduateEmployers.com
Register now for the latest news, local promotions, work experience and graduate vacancies at Baker Mckenzie.

BANK OF AMERICA

Bank of America knows being a great place to work for its employees is core to their success. While their teammates are focused on supporting clients and communities, Bank of America are focused on supporting teammates and their families, making sure they can be their best both at work and at home.

Bank of America welcomes graduates from all universities, degrees and backgrounds into its diverse and inclusive workplace. They firmly believe all employees should be treated with respect and be able to bring their whole selves to work. This is core to who they are as a company and how they drive responsible growth. Graduates can join Bank of America in areas including Audit, Research, Risk, Sales & Trading, Technology and more.

Each line of business offers unique opportunities, and there's plenty of collaboration across the bank designed to shape a smarter, greener, safer and more inclusive world. This includes everything from helping clients achieve sustainable growth and working with external partners to increase the number of women working in tech. As well as getting involved in exciting client projects, graduates are encouraged to make the most of the various internal groups and events such as sport and social club activities, employee network events and volunteering programmes.

Bank of America is committed to improving the environment in how they approach their global business strategy, work with partners, make their operations more sustainable, support their employees, manage risks and govern their activities. All of these opportunities give teammates the chance to shape a meaningful career, build connections both within and outside the bank and spend time on what matters to them.

Discover careers at Bank of America today.

GRADUATE VACANCIES IN 2023
ACCOUNTANCY
FINANCE
INVESTMENT BANKING
TECHNOLOGY

NUMBER OF VACANCIES
No fixed quota

LOCATIONS OF VACANCIES

Vacancies also available in Europe.

STARTING SALARY FOR 2023
£Competitive

WORK EXPERIENCE

| INSIGHT COURSES | DEGREE PLACEMENTS | SUMMER INTERNSHIPS |

UNIVERSITY PROMOTIONS DURING 2022-2023
BANGOR, BATH, BIRMINGHAM, BRISTOL, CAMBRIDGE, CARDIFF, CITY, DURHAM, EDINBURGH, EXETER, HULL, IMPERIAL COLLEGE LONDON, KING'S COLLEGE LONDON, LANCASTER, LEEDS, LEICESTER, LIVERPOOL, LONDON SCHOOL OF ECONOMICS, LOUGHBOROUGH, MANCHESTER, NEWCASTLE, NOTTINGHAM, OXFORD, QUEEN MARY LONDON, READING, ROYAL HOLLOWAY, SHEFFIELD, SOUTHAMPTON, ST ANDREWS, SURREY, UNIVERSITY COLLEGE LONDON, WARWICK, YORK
Please check with your university careers service for full details of Bank of America's local promotions and events.

MINIMUM ENTRY REQUIREMENTS
2.1 Degree

APPLICATION DEADLINE
Varies by function

FURTHER INFORMATION
www.Top100GraduateEmployers.com
*Register now for the latest news, local promotions, work experience and graduate vacancies at **Bank of America**.*

BBC

bbc.co.uk/youmakethebbc

@BBCGetIn 🐦 resourcing@bbc.co.uk ✉

@BBCGetIn 📷 linkedin.com/company/bbc in

The BBC is the world's leading public service broadcaster, producing distinctive, world-class programmes and content which inform, educate, and entertain millions of people in the UK and around the world. More than 20,000 staff work at the BBC in journalism, production, engineering, technology, and corporate services.

The BBC delivers content across the UK through a portfolio of television services, national and local radio networks, BBC World Service and a range of digital services.

With a strong focus on potential rather than the level of academic achievement, the BBC has graduate and postgraduate-level apprenticeship and trainee schemes across the board – schemes are available in Journalism, Content Production, Production Management, Broadcast Engineering, Software Engineering, Research and Development, UX Design, Marketing, Business and Corporate.

Programmes include a mix of working on placement on shows, products and services that are enjoyed every day by millions of people, with periods of training or day release.

New perspectives are important to the BBC, as is motivation for the role, attitude, curiosity and passion. Good communication skills, team working, creativity and ideas will strengthen applications.

The BBC's graduate apprenticeship and trainee schemes for 2023 are expected to open for applications from November 2022, with assessment centres taking place in early 2023 for a September start.

New opportunities do spring up throughout the year though, so interested students should register on the BBC's careers site and follow the BBC's social media to keep up-to-date with scheme opening dates.

GRADUATE VACANCIES IN 2023

ENGINEERING
FINANCE
HUMAN RESOURCES
LAW
MARKETING
MEDIA
RESEARCH & DEVELOPMENT
TECHNOLOGY

NUMBER OF VACANCIES
200+ graduate jobs

LOCATIONS OF VACANCIES

STARTING SALARY FOR 2023
£19,500-£23,842

WORK EXPERIENCE
INTERNSHIPS

UNIVERSITY PROMOTIONS DURING 2022-2023
Please check with your university careers service for full details of the BBC's local promotions and events.

MINIMUM ENTRY REQUIREMENTS
Varies by scheme

APPLICATION DEADLINE
Varies by scheme

FURTHER INFORMATION
www.Top100GraduateEmployers.com
Register now for the latest news, local promotions, work experience and graduate vacancies at the BBC.

Be part of something special. Join the BBC.

Opportunities in Broadcast Engineering, Software Engineering, Research & Development, User Experience, Journalism, Production and more.

To find out more, visit bbc.co.uk/youmakethebbc

When organisations find problems they can't solve on their own, that's where BCG gets to work. As the pioneer in business strategy consulting, it has been helping to solve some of the world's biggest problems since it was founded nearly 60 years ago. Today, its work is more fascinating than ever.

Graduates will join a 22,000-strong global team of consultants and subject-matter experts to partner with global clients on projects that make positive change happen. BCG helps organisations flourish in a world where sustainability is the priority. To date, BCG has enabled almost £2 billion in social impact consulting, and has made its own pledge to achieve net-zero climate impact by 2030.

Working at BCG, graduates will start making an impact on day one, with early exposure to the most senior leaders of global corporations. There are opportunities to build experience across different industries and sectors, and to work in projects at the forefront of technology, like advanced robotics, artificial intelligence, and blockchain.

This focus on the future means that BCG offers unparalleled opportunities for growth and development. The firm never stops learning: it continually invests in its employees with in-depth learning experiences, curated and led by senior BCGers and top-tier trainers from around the world.

BCG looks for bright students from any subject matter or discipline. It values people with high academic achievement, leadership skills, deep intellectual curiosity, and a problem-solving mindset. Diversity of thought, expertise, experience, and background are fundamental to BCG's success.

For graduates looking to continue their learning journey and make a real difference in the world, BCG is the place to start.

GRADUATE VACANCIES IN 2023
CONSULTING

NUMBER OF VACANCIES
No fixed quota

LOCATIONS OF VACANCIES

STARTING SALARY FOR 2023
£Competitive

WORK EXPERIENCE
SUMMER INTERNSHIPS

UNIVERSITY PROMOTIONS DURING 2022-2023
BATH, BIRMINGHAM, BRISTOL, CAMBRIDGE, CARDIFF, DURHAM, EDINBURGH, GLASGOW, IMPERIAL COLLEGE LONDON, KING'S COLLEGE LONDON, LEEDS, LIVERPOOL, LONDON SCHOOL OF ECONOMICS, MANCHESTER, NEWCASTLE, NOTTINGHAM, OXFORD, QUEEN MARY LONDON, SCHOOL OF AFRICAN STUDIES, SHEFFIELD, SOUTHAMPTON, ST ANDREWS, UNIVERSITY COLLEGE LONDON, WARWICK, YORK
Please check with your university careers service for full details of BCG's local promotions and events.

MINIMUM ENTRY REQUIREMENTS
2.1 Degree

APPLICATION DEADLINE
27th October 2022

FURTHER INFORMATION
www.Top100GraduateEmployers.com
Register now for the latest news, local promotions, work experience and graduate vacancies at BCG.

Design
the Future.
Welcome to
the Group.

BCG

Beyond consultants and business strategists, we are a network of data scientists, user experience designers, and experts across every field, industry, and region. We go beyond ideas to find solutions and put them into meaningful action. By helping our clients do amazing things, we help change the world.

careers.bcg.com

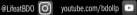

BDO

Accountancy and business advisory firm, BDO employs 7000 people across 18 offices in the UK, providing the solutions ambitious and entrepreneurial businesses need to navigate today's changing world. BDO UK is part of the BDO global network, providing advisory services in 164 countries.

When the most innovative and high-growth businesses need advice on accountancy and business, they turn to BDO. With expertise across Financial Services, Healthcare, Leisure and Hospitality, Retail, Manufacturing, Technology, Media, Not-for-Profit, Public Sector and many more industries, BDO provides the advice and answers that help AIM listed companies achieve their aspirations. Specialising in Tax, Audit and Assurance, Advisory, BDO's graduate programmes are for those who want to work with ambitious clients, on challenging work, from day one.

They look for trainees who want to bring themselves to everything they do. Those who are prepared to ask questions, offer up ideas and seize every opportunity. Those who have a drive to inspire more conversations and build lasting relationships. And in return, BDO will provide a breadth of experience and opportunities to develop skills that few could match.

Study for professional qualifications like the ACA, CFA and CTA to become an expert in a chosen area. At BDO, trainees are shaped into the independent and ethical advisors the UK's most forward-thinking businesses rely on. With early exposure to clients, trainees experience varied work that will broaden their horizons. BDO provides expert coaching and mentoring at every step, so that trainees can build a career with confidence.

Want to work at the very heart of accountancy and business?

Set a course for a rewarding career, with a role at BDO.

GRADUATE VACANCIES IN 2023
ACCOUNTANCY

NUMBER OF VACANCIES
700 graduate jobs

LOCATIONS OF VACANCIES

STARTING SALARY FOR 2023
£Competitive
Varies by region.

WORK EXPERIENCE
DEGREE PLACEMENTS | SUMMER INTERNSHIPS

UNIVERSITY PROMOTIONS DURING 2022-2023
ASTON, BIRMINGHAM, BRISTOL, CARDIFF, CITY, DURHAM, EDINBURGH, ESSEX, EXETER, GLASGOW, KING'S COLLEGE LONDON, LANCASTER, LEEDS, LEICESTER, LIVERPOOL, LONDON SCHOOL OF ECONOMICS, LOUGHBOROUGH, MANCHESTER, NEWCASTLE, NOTTINGHAM, NOTTINGHAM TRENT, READING, SHEFFIELD, SOUTHAMPTON, STRATHCLYDE, SURREY, SUSSEX, UNIVERSITY COLLEGE LONDON, WARWICK, YORK
Please check with your university careers service for full details of BDO's local promotions and events.

MINIMUM ENTRY REQUIREMENTS
Any degree accepted

APPLICATION DEADLINE
20th November 2022
Early application is advised.

FURTHER INFORMATION
www.Top100GraduateEmployers.com
Register now for the latest news, local promotions, work experience and graduate vacancies at BDO.

BlackRock

EMEACampusRecruitment@blackrock.com

@BlackRock — linkedin.com/company/blackrock

@BlackRock — youtube.com/blackrock

GRADUATE VACANCIES IN 2023

FINANCE
HUMAN RESOURCES
MARKETING
SALES
TECHNOLOGY

NUMBER OF VACANCIES
100+ graduate jobs

LOCATIONS OF VACANCIES

Vacancies also available in Europe.

STARTING SALARY FOR 2023
£Competitive

WORK EXPERIENCE

| INSIGHT COURSES | DEGREE PLACEMENTS | SUMMER INTERNSHIPS |

UNIVERSITY PROMOTIONS DURING 2022-2023
Please check with your university careers service for full details of BlackRock's local promotions and events.

APPLICATION DEADLINE
Varies by function

FURTHER INFORMATION
www.Top100GraduateEmployers.com
Register now for the latest news, local promotions, work experience and graduate vacancies at BlackRock.

BlackRock's purpose is to help more and more people experience financial well-being. As a global investment manager and leading provider of financial technology, their clients turn to them for the solutions needed when planning for their most important goals.

BlackRock is building a culture of innovation, curiosity and compassion, one that enables every employee to make an impact. Being a part of BlackRock means being a part of a community of smart, ambitious people. BlackRock values diversity of thought and background and believes everyone should have a voice at the table. No matter what level, employees are given real responsibility from day one – and BlackRock is looking for future colleagues to help challenge the status quo. BlackRock brings together financial leadership, worldwide reach and state-of-the-art technology to provide answers to the millions of investors who entrust their financial futures to the company.

The story of BlackRock's success rests not just with its founders, but with the thousands of talented people who have brought their ideas and energy to the firm every day since. That's why BlackRock is looking for fresh ideas and viewpoints. BlackRock knows that their continued success depends on their ability to use collective experiences and ideas to achieve more for their clients and the business. At BlackRock, students can have a career that's exciting, rewarding and full of possibilities and opportunities.

BlackRock offers roles in Analytics and Risk; Business Management and Strategy; Finance and Internal Audit; Human Resources; Investments; Legal and Compliance; Marketing and Communications; Sales and Relationship Management; and Technology. Whatever their background, whatever they're studying, there's a place for graduates at BlackRock.

BlackRock.

Let's invest in each other

BlackRock is a global investment manager and leading financial technology provider dedicated to helping more and more people experience financial well-being. The work we do for our clients moves markets, builds economies and supports millions of people around the globe as they save for their children's educations, home ownership or retirement.

To best serve our clients and meet their diverse needs around the world, we must bring forward an equally diverse range of perspectives and talent. It's why we're dedicated to creating an environment where our people feel welcomed, valued and supported with development opportunities, benefits and networks to help them thrive.

Explore opportunities at careers.blackrock.com/early-careers.

Stay connected @BlackRock

Bloomberg

As a global information and technology company, Bloomberg uses its dynamic network of data, ideas and analysis to solve difficult problems every day. Its customers around the world rely on them to deliver accurate, real-time business and market information that helps them make important financial decisions.

Bloomberg is guided by four core values: innovation, collaboration, customer service, and doing the right thing. The European Headquarters in London is a testament to that innovation, as it is the world's most sustainable office building.

Bloomberg offers insight weeks, internship and full-time entry-level roles at their London office across a range of business areas including Analytics & Sales, Data, Engineering, Operations and more. Candidates who join Bloomberg can build and define their own unique career, rather than a pre-defined path.

Bloomberg is proud to have a truly global dynamic organisation, so all employees are empowered to have an impact and are measured by their contributions. All graduate starters will participate in team-specific training that continues throughout their career via robust career development resources.

Bloomberg also offers internships to provide an unparalleled combination of learning, networking, and project responsibilities. The internship programme aims to provide first-hand exposure to its business and unique culture, and is filled with training, seminars, senior leader speaker series, philanthropic events, and much more.

Candidates apply online on Bloomberg's career website. The interview process will depend on the business area they have applied to, but typically involves a video and/or telephone interview followed by assessment days and in-person interviews. Bloomberg hire on a rolling basis, so early application is advised.

GRADUATE VACANCIES IN 2023
ENGINEERING
FINANCE
SALES
TECHNOLOGY
DATA

NUMBER OF VACANCIES
350+ graduate jobs

LOCATIONS OF VACANCIES

STARTING SALARY FOR 2023
£Competitive
Plus a competitive bonus.

WORK EXPERIENCE
INSIGHT COURSES SUMMER INTERNSHIPS

UNIVERSITY PROMOTIONS DURING 2022-2023
ASTON, BATH, BIRMINGHAM, BRISTOL, CAMBRIDGE, CITY, DURHAM, EDINBURGH, EXETER, GLASGOW, IMPERIAL COLLEGE LONDON, KING'S COLLEGE LONDON, LANCASTER, LONDON SCHOOL OF ECONOMICS, MANCHESTER, OXFORD, QUEEN MARY LONDON, SOUTHAMPTON, ST ANDREWS, STRATHCLYDE, UNIVERSITY COLLEGE LONDON, WARWICK
Please check with your university careers service for full details of Bloomberg's local promotions and events.

MINIMUM ENTRY REQUIREMENTS
Any degree accepted

APPLICATION DEADLINE
Year-round recruitment

FURTHER INFORMATION
www.Top100GraduateEmployers.com
*Register now for the latest news, local promotions, work experience and graduate vacancies at **Bloomberg**.*

Ready to join the workplace of the future?

Our London headquarters is waiting for you. Let's work on purpose. Together.

bloomberg.com/careers

Bloomberg

bp.com/grads/uk

bp delivers heat, light, and mobility products and services to customers around the world, and is doing so in ways that are helping drive the transition to a lower carbon future. The business employs over 63,600 people in operations in Europe, North and South America, Australasia, Asia, and Africa.

bp's purpose is to reimagine energy for people and the planet. To achieve this, bp is transforming its entire business. It's investing to grow renewable energy, expanding charging to support the growth of electric vehicles, and focusing its oil and gas business worldwide on higher quality and lower carbon operations.

This purpose is a driving force in bp, and it's shared by a global team. From engineers and scientists to traders and data analysts, they work together to drive the energy transformation. The professionals on bp's early talent programmes make an important contribution. Whether they are in business, digital, engineering, science, or trading, they bring their own ideas, ambitions, and perspectives to the table.

bp's internship and graduate programmes give new joiners a platform to achieve their full potential. Paid 11-week and year-long internships offer hands-on business experience to undergraduates or postgraduates who are about to start the final year of their degree or PhD. Graduates on their two- or three-year programmes gain a full range of skills and experience. And each programme is designed to open up a variety of opportunities and roles across bp.

Diverse and inclusive, bp's culture focuses on teamwork, respect, and ambition. Right from the start, students are offered a real chance to build a challenging, varied career and to contribute at any stage of the energy lifecycle. The result is a positive, supportive environment where everyone can achieve their ambitions while making a meaningful impact that reaches far beyond the business.

GRADUATE VACANCIES IN 2023

ENGINEERING
FINANCE
HUMAN RESOURCES
MARKETING
PURCHASING
RESEARCH & DEVELOPMENT
SALES
TECHNOLOGY

NUMBER OF VACANCIES
100+ graduate jobs

LOCATIONS OF VACANCIES

STARTING SALARY FOR 2023
£37,000-£48,000
Plus a £3,000-£5,000 settling-in allowance.

UNIVERSITY PROMOTIONS DURING 2022-2023
ABERDEEN, ASTON, BATH, BELFAST, BIRMINGHAM, CAMBRIDGE, DURHAM, HERIOT-WATT, IMPERIAL COLLEGE LONDON, LANCASTER, LEEDS, LEICESTER, LIVERPOOL, LONDON SCHOOL OF ECONOMICS, LOUGHBOROUGH, MANCHESTER, NEWCASTLE, NOTTINGHAM, OXFORD, SHEFFIELD, SOUTHAMPTON, STRATHCLYDE, SURREY, UNIVERSITY COLLEGE LONDON
Please check with your university careers service for full details of bp's local promotions and events.

MINIMUM ENTRY REQUIREMENTS
2.1 Degree

APPLICATION DEADLINE
Varies by function

FURTHER INFORMATION
www.Top100GraduateEmployers.com
Register now for the latest news, local promotions, work experience and graduate vacancies at bp.

Be part of reimagining *energy*

Intern and graduate opportunities in
Business | Digital | Engineering | Science | Trading

There's a lot to be part of at bp. We're reimagining energy and transforming our business – reducing our emissions, growing our low-carbon energy businesses, and forming partnerships around the world. Join us and you'll share this progress. You'll drive it too. Working with colleagues worldwide, you'll deliver projects that really matter and make an impact that reaches far beyond bp. To hear from some of the people behind our progress, follow us on social media. Or visit our careers site to see our opportunities and find out where you could fit in.

bp.com/grads/uk

bp

⟲ @ life.at.bp

🐦 @ bp_plc

f @ bpcareers

in @ bp

BT Group

bt.com/careers/early-careers

BTEarlyCareers   graduate.recruitment@bt.com
@BTEarlyCareers   linkedin.com/company/BT **in**
@BT_Careers 🖸   youtube.com/BTBetterFuture ▶

GRADUATE VACANCIES IN 2023
ENGINEERING
FINANCE
GENERAL MANAGEMENT
MARKETING
RESEARCH & DEVELOPMENT
SALES
TECHNOLOGY

NUMBER OF VACANCIES
250 graduate jobs

LOCATIONS OF VACANCIES

STARTING SALARY FOR 2023
£29,000-£35,000
Plus a 10% annual bonus.

WORK EXPERIENCE
| DEGREE PLACEMENTS | SUMMER INTERNSHIPS |

UNIVERSITY PROMOTIONS DURING 2022-2023
ASTON, BATH, BELFAST, BIRMINGHAM, BRISTOL, CAMBRIDGE, CARDIFF, CITY, DURHAM, EDINBURGH, ESSEX, EXETER, GLASGOW, IMPERIAL COLLEGE LONDON, KING'S COLLEGE LONDON, KENT, LEEDS, LEICESTER, LIVERPOOL, LONDON SCHOOL OF ECONOMICS, LOUGHBOROUGH, MANCHESTER, NEWCASTLE, NOTTINGHAM, NOTTINGHAM TRENT, OXFORD, QUEEN MARY LONDON, READING, SHEFFIELD, SOUTHAMPTON, UEA, UNIVERSITY COLLEGE LONDON, WARWICK

MINIMUM ENTRY REQUIREMENTS
2.1 Degree

APPLICATION DEADLINE
Please see website for full details.

FURTHER INFORMATION
www.Top100GraduateEmployers.com
Register now for the latest news, local promotions, work experience and graduate vacancies at BT Group.

BT Group is the global powerhouse behind EE, BT, Plusnet, and Openreach. This international business connects friends to family, clients to colleagues, people to possibilities. It keeps the wheels of business spinning, and the emergency services responding. And it uses the power of technology to help solve big challenges, like climate change and cyber security.

From day one, graduates will have a voice at BT Group. They'll get stuck in to tough challenges, pitch in with ideas, make things happen. They won't be alone: BT Group's managers and people will be there with help and support, learning and development. Graduates will make great friends, discover new talents, and feel part of something exhilarating.

BT Group values diversity and celebrates difference. Graduates are encouraged to be themselves, whatever their background. As Philip Jansen, BT Group's CEO, says: 'We embed diversity and inclusion into everything that we do. It's fundamental to our purpose: we connect for good.' Whichever brand people are working for, everyone is playing for the same team. And they all enjoy the rewards of being part of something bigger: the opportunities to explore new experiences, pursue different dreams, and climb challenging career ladders. BT Group is always looking ahead. The company doesn't just sell broadband, and networks, and security, and thousands of clever things most people have never heard of; in its Martlesham labs, BT is inventing the technologies of the future. For graduates wanting to sharpen their skills in digital, what better place than on the cutting edge?

Four brands. One team, 100,000 strong. Together, they're connecting the world. This is an opportunity for graduates to play their part in building the BT Group of the future, one that will be net zero by 2030.

BT Group

See the world in a different way.

You're yearning to make a difference to the world. You want to contribute to a global business that powers industry, fuels innovation, and connects us all. You want to do extraordinary things in a company with endless opportunities.

Join us and from day one you'll have a voice in one of the most dynamic companies in the UK. With real responsibility from the get-go, you'll pitch in with ideas and you'll make things happen.

And you'll learn, learn, learn, adding to your hard skills - like PRINCE2 Agile, Lean Six Sigma, or CIPD - and fluffing up the soft stuff, too, like adaptability, resilience, and creative thinking.

Our graduates tell us they love the support we give them, both on the job and through our graduate networks. They say it's 'outstanding'. They're right. You'll move around the company, meet clever people, soak up new influences, relish new challenges.

You could be diving into data analysis, creating dashboards, and learning how to keep your stakeholders on side. Or you're in HR, propelling our Diversity & Inclusion team to ever greater heights. Perhaps you're prepping the Annual General Meeting and briefing the CEO. Or maybe you're in Openreach, working out how engineers can use handheld testers to strengthen our network diagnostics.

We've got thousands of thrilling career opportunities

in every area of our business. Whatever your degree, you'll discover something exciting, challenging, and compelling at BT Group. And wherever you find yourself, you'll be contributing, making a difference.

Who knows, this time next year you could even be getting set to mentor a new graduate. But one thing is for certain – as a graduate with us, you'll feel wanted and appreciated.

There's no better place to be than BT Group for a fast-paced career with momentum, in a company that's fundamental to the fabric of the nation.

We're about more than just bottom line, we connect for good. And we'd like to connect with you.

Civil Service
Fast Stream

The Civil Service supports the government of the day to implement its policies effectively on behalf of every community across the UK. The award-winning Fast Stream leadership programme develops talented, high-potential graduates from all backgrounds to become the future leaders of the Civil Service.

This year, there will be a temporary pause on recruitment to the Fast Stream, while the Civil Service focuses on the Transformation Action Plan 2024. As part of a wider reform programme, work is being done to create a skilled and capable Civil Service, with high quality, relevant training and greater opportunities for all. In the meantime, the Civil Service will still be recruiting graduates to some of its departments, with opportunities in different locations across the UK. While not part of the Fast Stream, graduates recruited directly into departments will be supported by professional colleagues in a positive environment for growth and success.

Graduates are valued members of the wider Civil Service community, where people of all ages, cultures, and backgrounds develop their skills, knowledge and experience while helping to deliver vital public services and shape decisions that affect everyone's lives.

Students are also encouraged to apply for one of the Civil Service internships. These award-winning programmes offer a valuable opportunity to develop networks, build transferable skills and gain experience of working for the Civil Service before applying directly to a department, or to the Fast Stream when applications reopen in 2023.

The Civil Service Fast Stream is sharpening its focus on STEM subjects but will continue to provide opportunities for students across a broad range of degree subjects.

GRADUATE VACANCIES

ENGINEERING
FINANCE
GENERAL MANAGEMENT
HUMAN RESOURCES
PROPERTY
PURCHASING
RESEARCH & DEVELOPMENT
TECHNOLOGY

NUMBER OF VACANCIES
No fixed quota

LOCATIONS OF VACANCIES

STARTING SALARY
£28,000

WORK EXPERIENCE
SUMMER
INTERNSHIPS

**UNIVERSITY PROMOTIONS
DURING 2022-2023**
Please check with your university careers service for full details of the Civil Service's local promotions and events.

MINIMUM ENTRY REQUIREMENTS
2.2 Degree

APPLICATION DEADLINE
Reopening for applications from Autumn 2023.

FURTHER INFORMATION
www.Top100GraduateEmployers.com
Register now for the latest news, local promotions, work experience and graduate vacancies at the Civil Service.

Civil Service Fast Stream

FROM EDUCATION to test & trace TO TRANSPORT INNOVATION

COVID-19 Vaccination Centre

Graduate Leadership Development Programme

From science and engineering to digital and data to informing government policy with systems thinking, the Civil Service Fast Stream truly is You, Unlimited! Katie was thrilled when her first COVID-19 testing kit arrived, because she was part of the team working with the NHS to make it happen. And that was just one of her Fast Stream placements.

She's also worked with the Department for Education, Department for Transport, and next, it could be any one of a number of other Government Departments. Wherever Katie goes on the Fast Stream, she's ready to experience as much as possible. Are you? The Civil Service touches all aspects of UK life, and with a range of 15 different development schemes to choose from, you'll find there's something here for you – whatever your degree subject, background or age.

Explore more at faststream.gov.uk

You, unlimited.

CLYDE&CO

Clyde & Co has grown to become a leading law firm in its core industry sectors: Insurance, Energy, Marine & Natural Resources, Projects & Construction and Aviation. The firm offers a comprehensive range of legal services and advice to businesses operating at the heart of global trade and commerce.

From developed to emerging markets, Clyde & Co aims to support its clients by putting the power of the globally integrated firm at its disposal with a range of seamless and efficient services, and the very best, commercially minded legal advice.

For graduates looking for the perfect environment to learn, develop and progress, the London headquartered firm is the place to be. Clyde & Co boasts a range of opportunities for graduates across the globe; with a head count of over 5,000 staff operating from over 60 offices and associated offices across six continents. Whichever office graduates are in, and whichever scheme graduates choose to undertake, they can look forward to gaining some truly world class training taught by some of the most renowned associates and partners in the legal sector.

Diversity remains a strong focal point for the firm, and something that is at the heart of everything it does. Clyde & Co typically tends to work with very diverse clients; therefore it makes excellent business sense to also maintain a diverse workforce. The firm strongly believes that diversity is about tapping into different mindsets, celebrating individuality, and recognising that fresh perspectives can often open up new possibilities and opportunities.

Clyde & Co is a dynamic, rapidly expanding global law firm committed to operating in a responsible way. They are looking for talented, ambitious individuals to become part of their story.

GRADUATE VACANCIES IN 2023
LAW

NUMBER OF VACANCIES
75+ graduate jobs
For training contracts starting in 2025.

LOCATIONS OF VACANCIES

Vacancies also available worldwide.

STARTING SALARY FOR 2023
£26,500-£40,000

UNIVERSITY PROMOTIONS DURING 2022-2023
BRISTOL, DURHAM, EDINBURGH, EXETER, LANCASTER, LIVERPOOL, MANCHESTER, QUEEN MARY LONDON, SHEFFIELD
Please check with your university careers service for full details of Clyde & Co's local promotions and events.

MINIMUM ENTRY REQUIREMENTS
2.1 Degree

APPLICATION DEADLINE
Year-round recruitment

FURTHER INFORMATION
www.Top100GraduateEmployers.com
Register now for the latest news, local promotions, work experience and graduate vacancies at Clyde & Co.

CLYDE & CO

Become part of our story

Clyde & Co has grown to become a leading global law firm in our core sectors. With a headcount of over 5,000 staff operating from over 60 offices and associated offices across six continents, we offer a comprehensive range of legal services and advice to businesses operating at the heart of global trade and commerce.

law·tax·future

CMS is a future facing firm. Whether stakeholders are big or small, they always have the firm's full attention and expertise. In a world of ever-accelerating change where technology is increasingly important, their clear, business-focused advice helps clients of every size to face the future with confidence.

CMS is a full service law firm combining top quality sector expertise with international scale. They embrace technology and are committed to new ideas that challenge conventional ways of doing things. CMS puts the interests of clients at the heart of everything they do across 80+ offices in 40+ countries in the UK, Europe, the Middle East, Africa, Asia, and South America.

With more than 1,100 partners and 5,000 lawyers, CMS works in cross-border teams to deliver top quality, practical advice. The firm is recognised for its sector excellence and focus in consumer products; energy; financial institutions; hotels & leisure; infrastructure & projects; life sciences & healthcare; real estate; and technology, media & telecommunications.

When it comes to what they're looking for, keen intellect is vital, but CMS are looking for much more than academic qualifications. Whether applicants are law students, non-law students or career changers, the skills required include personal effectiveness, professional communication, drive for achievement and having a future facing outlook.

The main route to a training contract at CMS is by successfully completing the CMS Academy programme. Their two-year training contracts feature four six-month seats or national, international, or client secondments. CMS also offers insight to the firm through their First Steps programme, apprenticeships, widening participation work experience and scholarship opportunities, and the newly launched Business Development & Marketing Graduate Programme.

GRADUATE VACANCIES IN 2023
LAW

NUMBER OF VACANCIES
95 graduate jobs
For training contracts starting in 2025

LOCATIONS OF VACANCIES

Vacancies also available elsewhere in the world.

STARTING SALARY FOR 2023
£28,000-£50,000

WORK EXPERIENCE
SUMMER INTERNSHIPS

UNIVERSITY PROMOTIONS DURING 2022-2023
ABERDEEN, BATH, BIRMINGHAM, BRISTOL, CAMBRIDGE, CARDIFF, DUNDEE, DURHAM, EDINBURGH, EXETER, GLASGOW, LEEDS, LEICESTER, LONDON SCHOOL OF ECONOMICS, MANCHESTER, OXFORD, QUEEN MARY LONDON, SHEFFIELD, SOUTHAMPTON, STIRLING, STRATHCLYDE, WARWICK, YORK
Please check with your university careers service for full details of CMS's local promotions and events.

APPLICATION DEADLINE
24th December 2022

FURTHER INFORMATION
www.Top100GraduateEmployers.com
Register now for the latest news, local promotions, work experience and graduate vacancies at CMS.

CreditSuisse virtualemea.recruiting@credit-suisse.com

@CreditSuisse linkedin.com/company/credit-suisse

@CreditSuisse_Careers youtube.com/creditsuisse

Credit Suisse is a leading global wealth manager with strong investment banking capabilities. Headquartered in Zurich, Switzerland, its operation has a global reach and extends to about 50 countries worldwide across mature and emerging markets with more than 50,000 employees from over 150 different nations.

Credit Suisse partners across countries, divisions, and regions to deliver holistic financial solutions to their clients, including innovative products and specially tailored advice, aligned to their high ethical standards. They strive for quality and excellence in their work and professional relationships, recognising and rewarding extraordinary performance among employees and providing opportunities for internal mobility, dedicated training and leadership.

As a global and inclusive community, Credit Suisse benefit from a diverse range of perspectives to create value and drive results for their clients, shareholders, and communities. Their values are brought to life through the entrepreneurial spirit of all within their network. Credit Suisse offers graduates and interns best-in-class training, competitive benefits, and international expertise. Participants put what they have learned into practice and create a network among people who know the business. Employee development is their mission, and they are deeply committed to graduate and intern success.

Bring new-found knowledge and ambition to Credit Suisse's rewarding internships and graduate programmes. They provide a stimulating, welcoming working atmosphere so participants can learn from experts and make their mark in real-world tasks. The company build on their team spirit while celebrating their individual differences. Take advantage of an empowering environment, with challenges to help grow and colleagues that inspire. For graduates and students ready for a career lift-off, find a place with Credit Suisse.

GRADUATE VACANCIES IN 2023

FINANCE

INVESTMENT BANKING

TECHNOLOGY

NUMBER OF VACANCIES
200+ graduate jobs

LOCATIONS OF VACANCIES

Vacancies also available in Europe.

STARTING SALARY FOR 2023
£Competitive

WORK EXPERIENCE

| INSIGHT COURSES | DEGREE PLACEMENTS | SUMMER INTERNSHIPS |

UNIVERSITY PROMOTIONS DURING 2022-2023
BRISTOL, CAMBRIDGE, DURHAM, IMPERIAL COLLEGE LONDON, KING'S COLLEGE LONDON, KENT, LONDON SCHOOL OF ECONOMICS, LOUGHBOROUGH, NOTTINGHAM, OXFORD, QUEEN MARY LONDON, SOUTHAMPTON, ST ANDREWS, UNIVERSITY COLLEGE LONDON, WARWICK
Please check with your university careers service for full details of Credit Suisse's local promotions and events.

MINIMUM ENTRY REQUIREMENTS
2.1 Degree

APPLICATION DEADLINE
Varies by function

FURTHER INFORMATION
www.Top100GraduateEmployers.com
Register now for the latest news, local promotions, work experience and graduate vacancies at Credit Suisse.

Build for the future.
Influence tomorrow.

Our people are as important as the clients we serve. We foster a culture of excellence, made possible by our skilled, responsible and motivated employees. We recognize and reward outstanding performers, so they feel valued, trusted and excited.

**Discover a career at Credit Suisse
credit-suisse.com/campuscareers**

CREDIT SUISSE

Deloitte.

deloitte.co.uk/careers

DeloitteUK

@DeloitteCareers | linkedin.com/company/deloitte
@DeloitteCareersUK | youtube.com/DeloitteCareersUK

Deloitte makes its impact through collaboration. All around the world, their colleagues spark positive progress for their clients, people and society. Their curiosity creates all kinds of possibilities in the worlds of business and technology. There's a purpose here to believe in, and an impact that everyone can see.

From Human Capital, Tax Consulting, and Legal to Technology and Cyber, Deloitte is delivering end-to-end improvement programmes. They're turning disruption into opportunity, and redesigning Audit through automation. To do this, they're drawing on the strengths and perspectives of everyone in the business – including their graduates.

At Deloitte, graduates are supported to make a serious contribution to the projects and the business, in an environment where they can be their true selves, dream bigger, think creatively, and deliver real impact. And they can progress and learn every day – from the work they do, and the people they collaborate with.

It's not the background of graduates that matters here. It's their questioning minds, determination to make a difference, and eagerness to work with others to solve problems. These are the qualities that are embraced and developed at Deloitte. And with countless opportunities in different business areas, industries, and sectors, graduates will always find challenges that motivate and inspire them.

Deloitte has offices across the UK and Northern Ireland, including Aberdeen, Belfast, Cardiff, Channel Islands, London, Manchester, Reading, and many more. Wherever they join, graduates can be sure of joining a local and global business, with networks, connections, and shared values that reach right across the world.

Graduates at Deloitte can experience more, and go further. Join them, and create your own path.

GRADUATE VACANCIES IN 2023

ACCOUNTANCY
CONSULTING
FINANCE
HUMAN RESOURCES
LAW
PROPERTY
TECHNOLOGY

NUMBER OF VACANCIES
1,000+ graduate jobs

LOCATIONS OF VACANCIES

STARTING SALARY FOR 2023
£Competitive

WORK EXPERIENCE
INSIGHT COURSES | DEGREE PLACEMENTS | SUMMER INTERNSHIPS

UNIVERSITY PROMOTIONS DURING 2022-2023
Please check with your university careers service for full details of Deloitte's local promotions and events.

MINIMUM ENTRY REQUIREMENTS
2.1 Degree, 104 UCAS points
260 UCAS points for those who passed exams before 2017.

APPLICATION DEADLINE
Varies by function

FURTHER INFORMATION
www.Top100GraduateEmployers.com
Register now for the latest news, local promotions, work experience and graduate vacancies at Deloitte.

Deloitte.

Share our purpose.
Create your own path.

Choosing Deloitte means choosing opportunity.
The diversity of our business and the industries
we work in will offer you countless ways to
progress, contribute and shine. And whichever
path you take, we'll be right there with you.

What impact will you make?
deloitte.co.uk/students

Deutsche Bank is transforming the world of banking by bringing together new skills and different perspectives to innovate, progress and make a positive difference. Explore what a career in finance could look like with a variety of opportunities designed to help drive that change.

Each individual at Deutsche Bank has a part to play in reimagining banking services for corporations, governments and private individuals, worldwide. Everyone has real opportunities to drive economic growth, underpin societal progress and make a positive impact for the bank's clients, colleagues, investors and communities.

Every employee takes charge of their careers from day one. Joining a team that's truly global and connected will give an excellent foundation for an entire career. Graduates experience first-hand how the bank's inclusive and welcoming culture encourages everyone to bring their perspectives together to create innovative, tangible solutions with far-reaching impact. Ideas are heard, valued.

At Deutsche Bank, technology is the future. The innovative solutions the bank is delivering are redefining what can be achieved as a business. From updating and upgrading every system to creating own pioneering tools, the bank's technology teams are unlocking new possibilities that are being felt throughout the finance industry.

Deutsche Bank's development programme offers extensive training, exposure to stimulating projects, and the opportunity to gain the knowledge and skills needed to provide innovative products and services to their clients. For people ready to explore the true extent of their potential, Deutsche Bank is a place to gain exposure, see the bigger picture, and be inspired to challenge the status quo and drive change on a global scale.

GRADUATE VACANCIES IN 2023

FINANCE

INVESTMENT BANKING

TECHNOLOGY

NUMBER OF VACANCIES
100+ graduate jobs

LOCATIONS OF VACANCIES

Vacancies also available in Europe, Asia, the USA and elsewhere in the world.

STARTING SALARY FOR 2023
£Competitive
Plus a sign-on bonus.

WORK EXPERIENCE

| INSIGHT COURSES | DEGREE PLACEMENTS | SUMMER INTERNSHIPS |

UNIVERSITY PROMOTIONS DURING 2022-2023
ASTON, BATH, BIRMINGHAM, BRISTOL, CAMBRIDGE, CARDIFF, CITY, DURHAM, EDINBURGH, EXETER, GLASGOW, IMPERIAL COLLEGE LONDON, KING'S COLLEGE LONDON, KENT, LEEDS, LIVERPOOL, LONDON SCHOOL OF ECONOMICS, LOUGHBOROUGH, MANCHESTER, NOTTINGHAM, OXFORD, QUEEN MARY LONDON, READING, SHEFFIELD, SOUTHAMPTON, ST ANDREWS, SURREY, UNIVERSITY COLLEGE LONDON, WARWICK, YORK
Please check with your university careers service for full details of Deutsche Bank's local promotions and events.

MINIMUM ENTRY REQUIREMENTS
2.1 Degree

APPLICATION DEADLINE
Varies by function

FURTHER INFORMATION
www.Top100GraduateEmployers.com
*Register now for the latest news, local promotions, work experience and graduate vacancies at **Deutsche Bank**.*

Deutsche Bank
careers.db.com

Defining the future of finance.

Impactful work.
Feels like Deutsche Bank.

#PositiveImpact

dyson

GRADUATE VACANCIES IN 2023

ENGINEERING
FINANCE
HUMAN RESOURCES
MARKETING
RESEARCH & DEVELOPMENT
TECHNOLOGY

NUMBER OF VACANCIES
300 graduate jobs

LOCATIONS OF VACANCIES

Vacancies also available in Asia.

STARTING SALARY FOR 2023
£30,000
Plus additional benefits.

WORK EXPERIENCE

DEGREE PLACEMENTS   SUMMER INTERNSHIPS

UNIVERSITY PROMOTIONS DURING 2022-2023
Please check with your university careers service for full details of Dyson local promotions and events.

APPLICATION DEADLINE
Varies by function

FURTHER INFORMATION
www.Top100GraduateEmployers.com
Register now for the latest news, local promotions, work experience and graduate vacancies at Dyson.

Dyson is growing fast. In 2012, there were just 3,120 people – today, there are over 14,000. Dyson is focused on solving the problems that others ignore; solving them first using engineering and ingenuity. They're looking for people who have a passion for solving problems and for cutting-edge technology.

People who strive to create the future every single day by developing new things, different things, things that go against the grain with a diverse and global team of ingenious minds. Interns, graduates, and leaders at Dyson all look to the future, thinking about the most urgent problems and finding radical new ways to solve them. It means that Dyson's scale and size grow rapidly, making it rich in new opportunities. They value new ideas and diverse perspectives.

Dyson graduates are problem solvers and quick thinkers who have an insatiable curiosity and the ability to look at things differently. They quickly become part of a global network – a community that supports and learns from each other. With a mission-based approach to work, they gain invaluable exposure to the inner workings at Dyson through live projects with real challenges and real responsibility, getting the chance to make an impact on Dyson's future. Working alongside industry experts and senior leaders, they won't just learn how things are done, they'll find ways to make them better.

There's always plenty going on outside of the office, with a 140-strong cohort of graduates in 2022 alone. It's a fulfilling place to start working life within a community of people who inspire each other. They're looking for people to join teams across engineering, marketing, information technology, and more. People who share Dyson's core values and a passion for technology – those who won't settle for 'good enough' and can push the boundaries without fear and with abundant curiosity.

Embrace change.
Invent the future.
Rethinkers wanted.

careers.dyson.com/early-careers

Enterprise started life as a small business. Still family-owned, it's grown to be the largest global mobility provider in the world, with 10,000+ branches globally, an annual turnover of $23.9 billion and the biggest rental vehicle fleet on the planet. Join them and be one of the people driving this success.

From their senior leaders to their apprentices, Enterprise gives everyone the freedom to explore their potential, and the opportunities they need to rise to new challenges and take their skills to the next level – because their growth is what makes Enterprise's growth possible.

Nowhere is this philosophy better illustrated than in their approach to graduate careers. When people join their award-winning Management Training Programme, they empower them to start contributing right from the word go. It helps that they are divided up into smaller, local branches, so their graduates gain the skills and experience needed to run their own business in as little as two years.

As a Times Top 50 Employer for Women for 17 consecutive years running, Enterprise has created a work environment where women thrive and are encouraged to rise to new levels in their career, thanks to support of both management and their peers.

Enterprise is also still family-owned – their CEO Chrissy Taylor is the third generation of the Taylor family to run the company. This allows them to look forward even more confidently to the future, providing the stability they need to pursue the long-term good for their customers, their business and their employees, even in these challenging times. Join Enterprise on their Graduate Programme, and become one of the new generation helping them write the next chapter of their success story.

GRADUATE VACANCIES IN 2023
GENERAL MANAGEMENT
RETAIL
SALES

NUMBER OF VACANCIES
800+ graduate jobs

LOCATIONS OF VACANCIES

STARTING SALARY FOR 2023
£23,500
Plus performance-based bonuses once the graduate programme has been completed, and location allowance if applicable.

WORK EXPERIENCE
| DEGREE PLACEMENTS | SUMMER INTERNSHIPS |

UNIVERSITY PROMOTIONS DURING 2022-2023
ABERDEEN, ABERYSTWYTH, ASTON, BANGOR, BATH, BELFAST, BIRMINGHAM, BRADFORD, BRISTOL, BRUNEL, CAMBRIDGE, CARDIFF, CITY, DUNDEE, DURHAM, EDINBURGH, ESSEX, EXETER, GLASGOW, HERIOT-WATT, HULL, IMPERIAL COLLEGE LONDON, KEELE, KING'S COLLEGE LONDON, KENT, LANCASTER, LEEDS, LEICESTER, LIVERPOOL, LONDON SCHOOL OF ECONOMICS, LOUGHBOROUGH, MANCHESTER, NEWCASTLE, NORTHUMBRIA, NOTTINGHAM, NOTTINGHAM TRENT, OXFORD, OXFORD BROOKES, PLYMOUTH, QUEEN MARY LONDON, READING, ROYAL HOLLOWAY, SCHOOL OF AFRICAN STUDIES, SHEFFIELD, SOUTHAMPTON, ST ANDREWS, STIRLING, STRATHCLYDE, SURREY, SUSSEX, SWANSEA, UEA, ULSTER, UNIVERSITY COLLEGE LONDON, WARWICK, YORK

MINIMUM ENTRY REQUIREMENTS
Any degree accepted

APPLICATION DEADLINE
Year-round recruitment

FURTHER INFORMATION
www.Top100GraduateEmployers.com
Register now for the latest news, local promotions, work experience and graduate vacancies at Enterprise.

@EnterpriseRentaCar_Careers_UK   youtube.com/EnterpriseRentACarJobsandCareersEMEA
@ERAC_JOBS   linkedin.com/company/enterprise-rent-a-car

Your prospects

Do wonders for them as an
Intern or **Management Trainee**

What does a graduate career with the world's largest car rental company look like? It starts in one of our 10,000 branches worldwide. It continues with you becoming a manager of one of those branches, in as little as two years' time. From there, you can go in whatever direction you choose. National sales? Business rental? Human resources? The choice is yours. And whether you join us on our award-winning Management Trainee programme or as an Intern, you'll enjoy great benefits, excellent training and real responsibility from day one.

Discover more at
careers.enterprise.co.uk

enterprise

EVERSHEDS SUTHERLAND

eversheds-sutherland.com

gradrec@eversheds-sutherland.com ✉

ESLegalTrainee **f**   @ESLegalTrainee **○**   @ESLegalTrainee **y**

Eversheds Sutherland is a global law firm with more than 5,000 people across 35 countries. They're full-service with deep niche and sector experience. Whatever challenge, wherever in the world, they're equipped and ready to meet it. They live their values, they're purposeful and purpose-led.

Eversheds Sutherland are ambitious for their clients, their communities – and for their people. Whether starting out on their career or well established, whether a lawyer or in business services. If they're looking for what's next, Eversheds Sutherland are too.

Eversheds Sutherland focus on what needs to be done and they make it happen. This means working hard, going the extra mile, being themselves and making a difference, together. As the world changes, wherever graduates are in their career, they will progress with the firm. A global footprint, different practice and business areas, challenging matters, new technology and innovation that push their people and advance their careers. There's always something new and exciting to engage with. Graduates are encouraged to use their initiative, be creative and explore new things, in a growing, inspiring global firm. They're also flexible, friendly and respectful when this has never been more important.

They bring together different skillsets, global mindsets and approaches. They foster diversity of thought and the freedom to put ideas into action. They have an inherent respect for the individual. The only thing graduates must be is collaborative. Sharing ideas, asking questions, solving challenges and meeting their clients' goals: together. They're here because of, and for, their clients as well as for one another and they're one team.

Eversheds Sutherland: For what's next.

GRADUATE VACANCIES IN 2023
LAW

NUMBER OF VACANCIES
50 graduate jobs
For training contracts starting in 2025.

LOCATIONS OF VACANCIES

STARTING SALARY FOR 2023
£31,000-£44,000
*Starting salary dependant on region.
Plus a £5,000-£7,000 Maintenance
Grant when studying.*

WORK EXPERIENCE
SUMMER
INTERNSHIPS

**UNIVERSITY PROMOTIONS
DURING 2022-2023**
BIRMINGHAM, BRISTOL, CAMBRIDGE,
CARDIFF, DURHAM, KING'S COLLEGE
LONDON, LEEDS, LEICESTER, MANCHESTER,
NOTTINGHAM, OXFORD, QUEEN MARY
LONDON, UNIVERSITY COLLEGE LONDON
*Please check with your university careers
service for full details of Eversheds
Sutherland's local promotions and events.*

MINIMUM ENTRY REQUIREMENTS
2.1 Degree

APPLICATION DEADLINE
Varies by function

FURTHER INFORMATION
www.Top100GraduateEmployers.com
*Register now for the latest news, local
promotions, work experience and graduate
vacancies at **Eversheds Sutherland**.*

EVERSHEDS SUTHERLAND

Helping your future take off

Career opportunities across 73 global offices

2023 UK Summer Vacation Scheme:
Opening – 01/10/2022
Closing – 13/12/2022

2022 Graduate Insight Evenings:
Opening – 01/10/2022
Closing – 13/11/2022

2023 First Year Law/Second Year Non-Law Open Day:
Opening – 01/10/2022
Closing – 05/03/2023

2025 UK Training Contract:
Opening – 01/03/2023
Closing – 25/06/2023

2025 Middle East Training Contract:
Opening – 01/03/2023
Closing – 25/06/2023

2023 Hong Kong Summer Vacation Scheme:
Opening – 01/10/2022
Closing – 15/01/2023

2024 & 2025 Edinburgh Training Contract:
Opening – 01/03/2023
Closing – 25/06/2023

Apply online: **www.eversheds-sutherland.com/graduates/apply**

eversheds-sutherland.com

ey.com/uk/students

EYCareersUK
@EY_CareersUK linkedin.com/company/ernstandyoung
@EYUKcareers youtube.com/EYUKcareers

EY is one of the world's most influential professional services organisations. Operating across 150 countries with over 700 office locations, EY acts as a trusted partner to its clients, drawing upon fresh thinking and advanced technology to help make better business decisions.

With a clear purpose of building a better working world, EY believes that, by asking better questions, it can find better answers to some of today's most pressing issues. How can teams futureproof businesses? How will EY keep client data secure in a digital world filled with risk? How can EY colleagues take organisations to the next level in order to compete in the future? These are just a few of the questions that students could be tackling on one of EY's undergraduate or graduate programmes.

EY is home to some 300,000 people, who are each diverse and unique, with a breadth of passions and interests. What unites them is their curiosity. They find a sense of belonging at EY – not only because of its open and inclusive culture, but because everyone welcomes diverse perspectives and unique voices.

Whichever business area undergraduates and graduates join – Assurance, Consulting, Strategy and Transactions, or Tax – there's real scope for impact. Ideas will be welcomed and, across everything, they could harness the potential of pioneering technologies like artificial intelligence, machine learning, or robotic process automation. And with continued flexible working, they can work in EY's world, their way.

Students will have all the scope and autonomy needed to erase industry boundaries, to innovate, evolve, and thrive as they hone their skills on a broad range of local and global projects. This is an opportunity for them to be themselves, and become everything they ever wanted to be.

GRADUATE VACANCIES IN 2023

ACCOUNTANCY
CONSULTING
FINANCE
TECHNOLOGY

NUMBER OF VACANCIES
1,000+ graduate jobs

LOCATIONS OF VACANCIES

STARTING SALARY FOR 2023
£Competitive

WORK EXPERIENCE

INSIGHT COURSES	DEGREE PLACEMENTS	SUMMER INTERNSHIPS

UNIVERSITY PROMOTIONS DURING 2022-2023
ABERDEEN, ABERYSTWYTH, ASTON, BANGOR, BATH, BELFAST, BIRMINGHAM, BRADFORD, BRISTOL, BRUNEL, CAMBRIDGE, CARDIFF, CITY, DUNDEE, DURHAM, EDINBURGH, ESSEX, EXETER, GLASGOW, HERIOT-WATT, HULL, IMPERIAL COLLEGE LONDON, KEELE, KING'S COLLEGE LONDON, KENT, LANCASTER, LEEDS, LEICESTER, LIVERPOOL, LONDON SCHOOL OF ECONOMICS, LOUGHBOROUGH, MANCHESTER, NEWCASTLE, NORTHUMBRIA, NOTTINGHAM, NOTTINGHAM TRENT, OXFORD, OXFORD BROOKES, PLYMOUTH, QUEEN MARY LONDON, READING, ROYAL HOLLOWAY, SCHOOL OF AFRICAN STUDIES, SHEFFIELD, SOUTHAMPTON, ST ANDREWS, STIRLING, STRATHCLYDE, SURREY, SUSSEX, SWANSEA, UEA, ULSTER, UNIVERSITY COLLEGE LONDON, WARWICK, YORK

MINIMUM ENTRY REQUIREMENTS
Varies by function
Relevant degree required for some roles.

APPLICATION DEADLINE
Varies by function

FURTHER INFORMATION
www.Top100GraduateEmployers.com
Register now for the latest news, local promotions, work experience and graduate vacancies at EY.

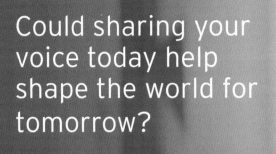

Could sharing your voice today help shape the world for tomorrow?

At EY, your curiosity can build the world we all imagine. Explore our school leaver, undergraduate and graduate programmes for a career that counts, an experience that challenges you and a team that empowers you to share your voice, whilst helping others find theirs.

Your career story is just beginning. We'll help you write it with the scale, teams and technology to build a career as unique as you are.

The exceptional EY experience. It's yours to build.

ey.com/uk/students

The better the question.
The better the answer.
The better the world works.

EY
Building a better
working world

freshfields.com/ukgraduates

FreshfieldsGraduates **f** ukgraduates@freshfields.com ✉

@FreshfieldsGrad **𝕐** linkedin.com/company/freshfields **in**

@FreshfieldsGrad 📷 youtube.com/FreshfieldsBruckhausDeringer ▶

Freshfields

At Freshfields graduates will be building the future, helping the world's biggest businesses, financial institutions and governments make the right decisions in a fast-changing world. Freshfields has a long history of innovation, and their award-winning legal advances keep their clients – and graduates – ahead of the curve.

Freshfields' unique eight-seat training contract gets graduates involved in high-profile, precedent-setting international work. Teamwork is central to their culture as they work across multiple geographical borders and practice groups. They have offices across the globe (including their newest in Silicon Valley), offering opportunities for secondments abroad. Freshfields' evolved working practices are a blend of remote and face-to-face office work, with support all the way until applicants qualify – and beyond.

They aim to have the greatest possible impact on access to justice through deep relationships with their pro bono clients and by pro-actively helping them in addressing systemic issues. As such, pro bono work is encouraged, supported and is fully accredited.

Freshfields see diversity as a strength and value fresh perspectives, creative ideas and connections. Graduates can expect to be collaborating with people who also bring different skills and experiences, working together to solve the most challenging legal problems. Honesty and support are prioritised at Freshfields: their trained Mental Health First aiders and other mental health initiatives are just one part of a much broader emphasis on wellbeing.

For individuals who are creative at problem-solving, curious about different ways of doing things, and a team player, Freshfields would love to hear from them.

GRADUATE VACANCIES IN 2023
LAW

NUMBER OF VACANCIES
90+ graduate jobs
For training contracts starting in 2025.

LOCATIONS OF VACANCIES

Vacancies also available in Asia.

STARTING SALARY FOR 2023
£50,000
Raising to £55,000 in 2nd Year of Training Contract and a NQ Salary of £125,000

WORK EXPERIENCE
INSIGHT COURSES | SUMMER INTERNSHIPS

UNIVERSITY PROMOTIONS DURING 2022-2023
Please check with your university careers service for full details of Freshfield's local promotions and events.

APPLICATION DEADLINE
Varies by function
Please see website for more details on Freshfield's range of Workshops, Vacation Schemes and Training Contracts.

FURTHER INFORMATION
www.Top100GraduateEmployers.com
Register now for the latest news, local promotions, work experience and graduate vacancies at Freshfields.

Expect more ▬

Go further with Freshfields

Apply now
freshfields.com/ukgraduates

Freshfields

Front|ine

Imagine a world where no child's life chances are limited by their social or family circumstance. That's the future Frontline is working towards. Frontline is a social work charity working to create social change for children in England without a safe or stable home, and for their families.

This is the work that 700,000 children in England rely on each year. These children need and deserve the support of life-changing social work professionals, who can empower them to achieve their full potential and help to break the cycle of trauma and disadvantage. That's why Frontline develops excellent social work practice, leadership and innovation.

This is the work where graduates will gain skills in leadership, conflict resolution, and relationship building. On the Frontline two-year programme they'll use these skills to bring about change inside the social work profession and beyond.

This is the work where people are the priority. Graduates will work directly with children and families, helping them make positive changes in their lives, qualifying as a social worker, and completing a fully-funded Master's degree.

This is the work where graduates will develop continuously. High-quality supervision and training from experienced social workers, academics, and coaches provide a rich, supportive environment for graduates to develop their professional skills and leadership. Graduates earn as they learn with a bursary in year one and a salary in year two.

This is the work where graduates will help create social change as part of the Frontline Fellowship: Frontline's national network of alumni, who receive continual support, training and funding to make a positive difference for children and families. This is the work. This is social work.

GRADUATE VACANCIES IN 2023
SOCIAL WORK

NUMBER OF VACANCIES
480 graduate jobs

LOCATIONS OF VACANCIES

STARTING SALARY FOR 2023
£18,000-£20,000
As a tax-free bursary in year one. Plus a fully-funded Master's degree.

WORK EXPERIENCE
SUMMER INTERNSHIPS

UNIVERSITY PROMOTIONS DURING 2022-2023
BIRMINGHAM, BRISTOL, CAMBRIDGE, DURHAM, EXETER, KING'S COLLEGE LONDON, LANCASTER, LEEDS, LIVERPOOL, MANCHESTER, NOTTINGHAM, OXFORD, QUEEN MARY LONDON, SHEFFIELD, WARWICK, YORK
Please check with your university careers service for full details of Frontline's local promotions and events.

MINIMUM ENTRY REQUIREMENTS
2.1 Degree

APPLICATION DEADLINE
Year-round recruitment
Early application is advised. Applications close for specific locations once vacancies are filled.

FURTHER INFORMATION
www.Top100GraduateEmployers.com
Register now for the latest news, local promotions, work experience and graduate vacancies at Frontline.

This is the work where you'll build the skills that help change lives

This is social work

Interested in a career that matters?
Apply to the Frontline programme today.

Front|ine

GRADUATE VACANCIES IN 2023

ENGINEERING

GENERAL MANAGEMENT

INTELLIGENCE GATHERING

RESEARCH & DEVELOPMENT

TECHNOLOGY

NUMBER OF VACANCIES
200+ graduate jobs

LOCATIONS OF VACANCIES

STARTING SALARY FOR 2023
£30,000+

WORK EXPERIENCE

INSIGHT COURSES | DEGREE PLACEMENTS | SUMMER INTERNSHIPS

UNIVERSITY PROMOTIONS DURING 2022-2023
Please check with your university careers service for full details of GCHQ's local promotions and events.

MINIMUM ENTRY REQUIREMENTS
Varies by function
Relevant degree required for some roles.

APPLICATION DEADLINE
Varies by function

FURTHER INFORMATION
www.Top100GraduateEmployers.com
Register now for the latest news, local promotions, work experience and graduate vacancies at GCHQ.

Government Communications Headquarters (GCHQ) is the UK's signals intelligence and cyber security agency. It works alongside MI5 and SIS (MI6) to keep the UK and its citizens safe at home, overseas and online. Using cutting-edge technology and technical ingenuity, GCHQ's mission is to counter threats including terrorism, espionage, organised crime, and cyber-attacks.

GCHQ is looking for graduates with different skills, backgrounds, and perspectives to help protect the UK. There are a range of graduate roles available in areas including technology, maths, language, analysis, and project management. Students can take advantage of a variety of paid summer placements in cyber, maths, and languages. Bursaries are also available to students studying any degree who have an interest in cyber security. Graduates joining GCHQ can expect challenging projects, outstanding professional development, and a rewarding career experience.

GCHQ is proud of its mission and its people. Its working culture encourages open minds and attitudes and is supported by a welfare and benefits structure that enables its workforce to be at its best. From extensive training and development that helps employees expand their skills to flexible working patterns that support a healthy work-life balance, GCHQ seeks to create an environment where everyone can achieve their full potential.

Applications are welcome from everyone, regardless of age, experience, cultural background, and sexual orientation. Due to the sensitive nature of the work, there are strict nationality, residency, and security requirements, and all applicants will be subject to a rigorous but fair vetting process. Applicants will need to be British citizens and need to have lived in the UK for seven out of the last ten years before applying, although some exceptions may apply.

WITH THE RIGHT MIX OF MINDS, ANYTHING IS POSSIBLE.

At GCHQ, we have a clear purpose - we want to help protect the UK. We work against cyber-attacks, terrorism and espionage. It's unique work that relies on people with unique perspectives. That's why we'll never ask you to be anything other than yourself. For us, having a diverse workforce isn't a box ticking exercise, it's an essential part of keeping the UK safe.

To find out more about our variety of roles, please visit **www.gchq-careers.co.uk**

@GCHQ   @GCHQ   GCHQ

UK 300 | Stonewall DIVERSITY CHAMPION 2021/22   disability confident LEADER

Goldman Sachs is a leading global financial services firm providing investment banking, securities, and investment management services to a substantial and diversified client base that includes corporations, financial institutions, governments, and individuals.

Goldman Sachs seeks out people with all types of skills, interests and experiences. There's no template for the "right" Goldman Sachs employee, which is why they search for talent in new places and in new ways, seeking different majors, personalities, experiences, skills, and working styles.

For them, it's all about bringing together people who are curious, collaborative, and have the drive to make things possible for their clients and communities.

With 70+ offices and 36,000+ people, Goldman Sachs is constantly evolving and innovating to shape the future of finance and to help its clients in an ever-changing world.

The Goldman Sachs culture fosters an environment that enables colleagues to fulfil their highest aspirations, both professionally and personally. From digital learning and leadership development training to resilience and mindfulness offerings, they are invested in all aspects of their workforce and are committed to growth at every level.

At Goldman Sachs, their goal is to attract the extraordinarily talented and diverse people needed to drive their business into the future. Diversity and inclusion is a business imperative and they strive to cultivate a work experience where their people can reach their full potential and thrive as their authentic selves. For Goldman Sachs' people to excel, everyone must feel that they are operating in an inclusive environment that celebrates differences and values different ways of thinking.

GRADUATE VACANCIES IN 2023

ACCOUNTANCY
ENGINEERING
FINANCE
HUMAN RESOURCES
INVESTMENT BANKING
LAW
RESEARCH & DEVELOPMENT
SALES
TECHNOLOGY

NUMBER OF VACANCIES
400 graduate jobs

LOCATIONS OF VACANCIES

STARTING SALARY FOR 2023
£Competitive
Competitive bonus and relocation allowance.

WORK EXPERIENCE

| INSIGHT COURSES | DEGREE PLACEMENTS | SUMMER INTERNSHIPS |

UNIVERSITY PROMOTIONS DURING 2022-2023
ASTON, BATH, BIRMINGHAM, BRADFORD, BRISTOL, CAMBRIDGE, CARDIFF, CITY, EDINBURGH, ESSEX, EXETER, GLASGOW, IMPERIAL COLLEGE LONDON, KING'S COLLEGE LONDON, LANCASTER, LEEDS, LEICESTER, LONDON SCHOOL OF ECONOMICS, LOUGHBOROUGH, MANCHESTER, NEWCASTLE, NOTTINGHAM, OXFORD, QUEEN MARY LONDON, ROYAL HOLLOWAY, SHEFFIELD, SOUTHAMPTON, ST ANDREWS, SURREY, UNIVERSITY COLLEGE LONDON, WARWICK, YORK

MINIMUM ENTRY REQUIREMENTS
Any degree accepted

APPLICATION DEADLINE
20th November 2022

FURTHER INFORMATION
www.Top100GraduateEmployers.com
Register now for the latest news, local promotions, work experience and graduate vacancies at Goldman Sachs.

Curious, collaborative and driven?
Let's chat.

See yourself here.

At Goldman Sachs, we believe who you are makes you better at what you do. We seek out people with all types of skills, interests and experiences. Even if you have never imagined a career in finance, there's a place for you here. For us, it's all about bringing together people who are curious, collaborative and have the drive to make things possible for our clients and communities. Interested? We'd love to meet you –join us at our upcoming events or programmes to meet us and learn more about our opportunities.

EMEA APPLICATION DEADLINES
We review applications on a rolling basis and encourage you to apply as soon as you are ready

20 November 2022
- New Analyst Programme (excl. Engineering / Warsaw)
- Summer Analyst Programme (excl. Engineering / Warsaw)
- Spring Programme
- Work Placement Programme

31 January 2023
- Engineering New Analyst & Summer Analyst

26 February 2023
- Degree Apprenticeship Programmes

Rolling Deadlines*
- Warsaw (All Programmes)
- Off-Cycle Internships
- Goldman Sachs Insight Events & Exploratory Programmes

Make things possible.

*If you're a professional with 1-3 years of experience, you may be eligible for our Early Careers opportunities. Please visit **GS.com/careers/professionals/early-careers** for further information.

Goldman
Sachs

GoldmanSachs.com/Careers

Google

Larry Page and Sergey Brin founded Google in September 1998 with a mission to organise the world's information and make it universally accessible and useful. Since then, the company has grown to more than 120,000 employees worldwide, with a wide range of popular products and platforms.

A problem isn't truly solved until it's solved for all.

Googlers build products that help create opportunities for everyone, whether down the street or across the globe. They bring insight, imagination, and a healthy disregard for the impossible. They bring everything that makes them unique. It's really the people that make Google the kind of company it is. Google hires people who are smart and determined, and favours their ability over their experience.

Google hires graduates from all disciplines, from humanities and business-related courses to engineering and computer science. The ideal candidate is someone who can demonstrate a passion for the online industry and someone who has made the most of their time at university through involvement in clubs, societies, or relevant internships. Google hires graduates who have a variety of strengths and passions, not just isolated skill sets. For technical roles within engineering teams, specific skills will be required. The diversity of perspectives, ideas, and cultures – both within Google and in the tech industry overall – leads to the creation of better products and services.

Whether it's providing online marketing consultancy, selling an advertising solution to clients, hiring the next generation of Googlers, or building products, Google has full-time roles and internships available across teams like global customer solutions, sales, people operations, legal, finance, operations, cloud, and engineering.

GRADUATE VACANCIES IN 2023
CONSULTING
ENGINEERING
HUMAN RESOURCES
MARKETING
SALES
TECHNOLOGY

NUMBER OF VACANCIES
No fixed quota

LOCATIONS OF VACANCIES

Vacancies also available in Europe.

STARTING SALARY FOR 2023
£Competitive

WORK EXPERIENCE
SUMMER
INTERNSHIPS

UNIVERSITY PROMOTIONS DURING 2022-2023
Please check with your university careers service for full details of Google's local promotions and events.

MINIMUM ENTRY REQUIREMENTS
Relevant degree required for some roles.

APPLICATION DEADLINE
Year-round recruitment

FURTHER INFORMATION
www.Top100GraduateEmployers.com
Register now for the latest news, local promotions, work experience and graduate vacancies at Google.

Build for everyone

Together, we can create opportunities for people to learn, be heard, and succeed.
google.com/students

Google

Grant Thornton

GRADUATE VACANCIES IN 2023
ACCOUNTANCY
CONSULTING
FINANCE

NUMBER OF VACANCIES
350-400 graduate jobs

LOCATIONS OF VACANCIES

STARTING SALARY FOR 2023
£Competitive

WORK EXPERIENCE
DEGREE PLACEMENTS | SUMMER INTERNSHIPS

UNIVERSITY PROMOTIONS DURING 2022-2023
Please check with your university careers service for full details of Grant Thornton's local promotions and events.

MINIMUM ENTRY REQUIREMENTS
Any degree accepted

APPLICATION DEADLINE
Year-round recruitment
Early application is advised.

FURTHER INFORMATION
www.Top100GraduateEmployers.com
Register now for the latest news, local promotions, work experience and graduate vacancies at Grant Thornton.

As one of the world's leading independent audit, tax and advisory firms, Grant Thornton is a team of independent thinkers who put quality, inclusion and integrity first. Offering a different perspective to their clients all around the world. A better experience. Delivering expertise in a way that goes beyond.

Embracing uniqueness, the culture at Grant Thornton thrives on the contributions of all the people who work there – they never settle for what is easy, and they look beyond to deliver the right thing, for everyone.

On the Grant Thornton graduate programme, there's training and support to start thriving in no time. Within three years, graduates become professionally qualified, specialising in either audit, tax or advisory.

Covering the full range of clients, experiences are truly there for the taking. And with exposure to clients from early on in their career, trainees take on real responsibility and benefit from the knowledge and experience of colleagues.

Grant Thornton's open and accessible culture gives trainees amazing opportunities to interact with senior business figures early in their career, and – with support from managers and exceptional training opportunities – the firm will do everything they can to help build the foundations for a great career.

Once qualified, the opportunities for graduates open up even further. They can keep progressing in their team, explore a different business area, or travel abroad and work at one of the 130+ Grant Thornton member firms around the world. The firm care more about an individual's potential than academic achievements alone, helping to get graduates' working lives off to a flying start. Grant Thornton is looking for people who can add value, spark fresh ideas and go beyond expectations. People that want to be able to proudly do what's right – for the firm, their colleagues, and their clients. It's how it should be.

GREAT MINDS. NOTHING ALIKE.

If they were, we wouldn't be where we are today. Difference of opinion is something we celebrate, and we'll back you so you can back yourself. Freeing up your time and energy to unlock ideas and innovations that propel our clients, and your career, forward. We value your potential as much as your academic achievements. **It's how it should be.**

Audit | Tax | Advisory

Visit **trainees.grantthornton.co.uk** to learn more

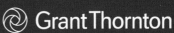

GSK

GSK is a global biopharma company with a special purpose –
to unite science, technology and talent to get ahead of disease
together. They do this by positively impacting the health
of billions of people, delivering stronger, more sustainable
shareholder returns as an organisation where people can thrive.

GSK's focus is to deliver a new generation of vaccines and medicines using the
science of the immune system, human genetics and advanced technologies to
get ahead of infectious diseases, HIV, cancer and other immune-mediated and
respiratory diseases. They do all this with a commitment to operate responsibly
for all their stakeholders by prioritising Innovation, Performance and Trust. Their
bold ambitions for patients are reflected in new commitments to growth and a
significant step-change in delivery over the next five years. This means more
GSK vaccines and medicines, including innovative new products, will reach more
people who need them than ever before.

GSK have long believed that building trust is key to stronger performance,
helping to create value for shareholders, impact for patients and society and a
reason outstanding people choose to work for and with them. That's why being
a responsible business is an integral part of the GSK strategy. Taking action on
environmental, social and governance issues is a key driver in their strategy.

The success of GSK absolutely depends on its people. While getting ahead of
disease together is about their ambition for patients and shareholders, it's also
about making GSK a place where people can thrive. GSK wants to be a place
where people feel inspired, encouraged and challenged to be the best they can
be. A place where they can be themselves – feel welcomed, valued and included.
Where they can keep growing and look after their wellbeing.

Join GSK at this exciting moment in their journey, to get Ahead Together.

GRADUATE VACANCIES IN 2023
ENGINEERING
FINANCE
HUMAN RESOURCES
LOGISTICS
MARKETING
PURCHASING
RESEARCH & DEVELOPMENT
SALES
TECHNOLOGY

NUMBER OF VACANCIES
35+ graduate jobs

LOCATIONS OF VACANCIES

Vacancies also available worldwide.

STARTING SALARY FOR 2023
£31,400
*Plus an annual bonus, private healthcare
and other perks.*

WORK EXPERIENCE
DEGREE PLACEMENTS   SUMMER INTERNSHIPS

UNIVERSITY PROMOTIONS
DURING 2022-2023
*Please check with your university careers
service for full details of GSK's local
promotions and events.*

APPLICATION DEADLINE
**September -
November 2022**

FURTHER INFORMATION
www.Top100GraduateEmployers.com
*Register now for the latest news, local
promotions, work experience and
graduate vacancies at GSK.*

HAL=ON

Our leading consumer brands.

SENSODYNE · Voltaren · parodontax · POLIDENT · Panadol · Advil · Otrivin · THERAFLU · Centrum

Haleon's portfolio of category-leading brands previously formed the Consumer Healthcare division of global biopharma company GSK. As of Monday 18 July 2022, Haleon began its journey as an independent global leader which is 100 per cent focused on everyday health.

In front of Haleon is an incredible opportunity. To deliver better everyday health with humanity. An invitation to make it more achievable, more inclusive, and more sustainable. Together, Haleon are empowering millions of people worldwide to take more control of their own health.

To do this, the company is committed to building on their global portfolio of category-leading brands like Sensodyne, Panadol and Voltaren. To combine their trusted science with deep human understanding. And to go beyond everything they've done before. Early talent roles at Haleon offer the chance to change the way people see and manage their everyday health. It's a unique opportunity. An exciting challenge. And a huge responsibility.

Haleon are always looking for ambitious apprentices, students and graduates who are inspired by their purpose and share their passion for helping people make a difference to their everyday health. Through their early talent opportunities, graduates will get an incredible insight into how Haleon works. They vary by region and function, but wherever graduates join, they'll build strong leadership capabilities. They'll be coached in the skills they need to succeed now and in the future. And they'll be stretched and challenged so they can go beyond what they thought they were capable of. Often the best way to find out what you want to do in the future is to experiment. By stepping into different teams, challenges, and environments. Haleon's work experience, internships and placements will give graduates just that.

GRADUATE VACANCIES IN 2023
ENGINEERING
FINANCE
HUMAN RESOURCES
LOGISTICS
MARKETING
PURCHASING
RESEARCH & DEVELOPMENT
SALES
TECHNOLOGY

NUMBER OF VACANCIES
20+ graduate jobs

LOCATIONS OF VACANCIES

STARTING SALARY FOR 2023
£31,000+
Plus competitive bonuses

WORK EXPERIENCE
INSIGHT COURSES | SUMMER INTERNSHIPS

MINIMUM ENTRY REQUIREMENTS
Varies by function
Relevant degree required for some roles.

UNIVERSITY PROMOTIONS DURING 2022-2023
Please check with your university careers service for full details of Haleon's local promotions and events.

APPLICATION DEADLINE
Varies by function

FURTHER INFORMATION
www.Top100GraduateEmployers.com
Register now for the latest news, local promotions, work experience and graduate vacancies at Haleon.

HALEON

Take ~~steps~~
strides.

For Health. With Humanity.

Care to join us. **haleon.com/careers**

uk.graduaterecruitment@hsbc.com

HSBCCareers f   linkedin.com/company/hsbc in

@lifeatHSBC   youtube.com/lifeatHSBC

HSBC

GRADUATE VACANCIES IN 2023

FINANCE

GENERAL MANAGEMENT

INVESTMENT BANKING

TECHNOLOGY

NUMBER OF VACANCIES
600+ graduate jobs

LOCATIONS OF VACANCIES

Vacancies also available worldwide.

STARTING SALARY FOR 2023
£Competitve
Plus bonuses.

WORK EXPERIENCE

| INSIGHT COURSES | DEGREE PLACEMENTS | SUMMER INTERNSHIPS |

UNIVERSITY PROMOTIONS DURING 2022-2023
ABERDEEN, ABERYSTWYTH, ASTON, BANGOR, BATH, BELFAST, BIRMINGHAM, BRADFORD, BRISTOL, BRUNEL, CAMBRIDGE, CARDIFF, CITY, DUNDEE, DURHAM, EDINBURGH, ESSEX, EXETER, GLASGOW, HERIOT-WATT, HULL, IMPERIAL COLLEGE LONDON, KEELE, KING'S COLLEGE LONDON, KENT, LANCASTER, LEEDS, LEICESTER, LIVERPOOL, LONDON SCHOOL OF ECONOMICS, LOUGHBOROUGH, MANCHESTER, NEWCASTLE, NORTHUMBRIA, NOTTINGHAM, NOTTINGHAM TRENT, OXFORD, OXFORD BROOKES, PLYMOUTH, QUEEN MARY LONDON, READING, ROYAL HOLLOWAY, SCHOOL OF AFRICAN STUDIES, SHEFFIELD, SOUTHAMPTON, ST ANDREWS, STIRLING, STRATHCLYDE, SURREY, SUSSEX, SWANSEA, UEA, ULSTER, UNIVERSITY COLLEGE LONDON, WARWICK, YORK

MINIMUM ENTRY REQUIREMENTS
Varies by function
Relevant degree required for some roles.

APPLICATION DEADLINE
Varies by function

FURTHER INFORMATION
www.Top100GraduateEmployers.com
Register now for the latest news, local promotions, work experience and graduate vacancies at HSBC.

With a global network across 63 countries and territories, serving more than 40 million customers, HSBC is one of the world's largest and most connected banking and financial services organisations. It is focused on opening up a world of opportunity.

HSBC is looking for students and graduates who are collaborative in action and curious thinkers – individuals with the courage to challenge the status quo and the motivation to make a positive impact for the customers they serve and the communities in which they operate.

HSBC is focused on building a sustainable future and serving the needs of a changing world. The company knows that economic growth must be sustainable for colleagues, customers, and communities. HSBC is focused on the importance of providing sustainable financial solutions to support customers in their transition to net zero – all while speeding up its own transition to becoming a net zero bank.

HSBC puts diversity at the heart of its business and provides an open, supportive, and inclusive working environment, with tailored training and support to help employees thrive on their chosen career path. No matter what interests and skills they might have, a career at HSBC will offer the opportunities, experiences, networks, and training needed – so there's no limit to how far they can go as part of an international and connected workforce.

Students and graduates can apply to join HSBC's local or global intern and graduate programmes across the bank in the following areas: Commercial Banking, Global Banking & Markets, Wealth and Personal Banking (including Global Asset Management and Private Banking), or Digital Business Services, including Operations and Technology.

Do great minds
think alike

or completely
differently?

At HSBC, diversity isn't a buzzword.
It's essential. That's why we encourage
applications to our Global Internships
and Graduate Programmes from
students and graduates with any
degree, from any background.

hsbc.com/earlycareers

 HSBC

J.P.Morgan

jpmorgan.com/careers

J.P. Morgan are committed to helping businesses and markets grow and develop in more than 100 countries. Over the last 200 years, they have evolved to meet the complex financial needs of some of the world's largest companies, as well as many of the smaller businesses driving industry change.

J.P. Morgan work hard to do the right thing for their clients, shareholders, and the firm every day. Joining the firm means learning from experts in a collaborative team environment where successful applicants will be supported to make an immediate impact from the start.

Whilst academic achievements are important, they're also looking for individuality and passion, as demonstrated by extra-curricular activities. J.P. Morgan invest in helping graduates fulfil their potential as they build their career at the firm. Internship and graduate positions are available firmwide, so applicants are encouraged to learn as much as possible about the different business areas and roles. They also offer pre-internship programmes, such as Early Insights, which provide insight into the finance industry and their programmes. They often hire directly from these opportunities – giving successful applicants early exposure to the firm and how they do business. The internship and full-time programmes they hire into are: asset management, corporate analyst development, data science & machine learning, global finance & business management, human resources, investment banking, markets, quantitative research, risk, software engineer, tech connect, wealth management, wholesale payments, and corporate banking.

Working with a team committed to doing their best, earning the trust of their clients, and encouraging employees to fulfil their potential – that's what it means to be part of J.P. Morgan.

GRADUATE VACANCIES IN 2023
ACCOUNTANCY
CONSULTING
FINANCE
GENERAL MANAGEMENT
HUMAN RESOURCES
INVESTMENT BANKING
RESEARCH & DEVELOPMENT
SALES
TECHNOLOGY

NUMBER OF VACANCIES
500 graduate jobs

LOCATIONS OF VACANCIES

Vacancies also available in Europe, Asia, the USA and elsewhere in the world..

STARTING SALARY FOR 2023
£Competitive
Annual competitive bonus.

WORK EXPERIENCE
INSIGHT COURSES | DEGREE PLACEMENTS | SUMMER INTERNSHIPS

UNIVERSITY PROMOTIONS DURING 2022-2023
ABERDEEN, ASTON, BATH, BELFAST, BIRMINGHAM, BRISTOL, CAMBRIDGE, CARDIFF, DURHAM, EDINBURGH, EXETER, GLASGOW, HERIOT-WATT, IMPERIAL COLLEGE LONDON, KING'S COLLEGE LONDON, LONDON SCHOOL OF ECONOMICS, MANCHESTER, OXFORD, PLYMOUTH, QUEEN MARY LONDON, SOUTHAMPTON, ST ANDREWS, STIRLING, STRATHCLYDE, UNIVERSITY COLLEGE LONDON, WARWICK

APPLICATION DEADLINE
27th November 2022

FURTHER INFORMATION
www.Top100GraduateEmployers.com
Register now for the latest news, local promotions, work experience and graduate vacancies at J.P Morgan..

J.P.Morgan

Choose a career with choice

We're looking for students from all majors and backgrounds to join our diverse, global team.

As a top employer in financial services, J.P. Morgan does much more than manage money. Here, you'll have more chances to continuously innovate, learn and make a positive impact for our clients, customers and communities.

We offer internships in over 12 different business areas as well as Early Insight Programs to introduce you to the industry and our company.

jpmorgan.com/careers

Biko | Automated Trading   **Susan** | Strategy Associate   **Ami** | Equity Research Associate

KPMG

kpmgcareers.co.uk

KPMGrecruitment **f**   graduate@kpmg.co.uk **✉**

@KPMGrecruitment **𝕏**   linkedin.com/company/kpmg-advisory **in**

@KPMGtraineesUK **⊙**   youtube.com/KPMGrecruitmentUK **▶**

KPMG in the UK is part of a global network of member firms that offers Audit, Consulting, Deal Advisory, Tax & Law and Technology services. Through the talent of over 15,000 people, the firm turns insights into opportunities, making a positive difference for their clients and the communities they serve.

KPMG's largest practice is Audit, which helps to build trust in businesses and the economy and has a relentless focus on audit quality. In Consulting, Deal Advisory, Tax & Law and Technology & Engineering, KPMG helps companies solve challenges, transforms businesses, develops confidence in markets and builds stronger communities.

Like the organisations they work with, KPMG is truly embracing change and is creating a tech-driven, sustainable business that empowers their people to be outstanding in delivery and has a lasting impact on the world.

KPMG is committed to creating an inclusive community where people can come as they are and thrive. It's known for its collaborative culture, with people who take care of each other and bring their unique experiences and perspectives to build a better future together.

Trainees at KPMG have the chance to work with some of the brightest minds on emerging practices and technologies. They benefit from structured development, including funded professional qualifications or accreditations, gaining learning for a lifetime. Through a broad range of KPMG employee networks, volunteering, and community initiatives, trainees are encouraged to build relationships and make an impact outside of their day-job too.

Joining KPMG means working for a values-led firm that supports people to be their best and make their mark, empowering people to build the career they want.

GRADUATE VACANCIES IN 2023

ACCOUNTANCY

CONSULTING

FINANCE

GENERAL MANAGEMENT

LAW

TECHNOLOGY

NUMBER OF VACANCIES
1,000+ graduate jobs

LOCATIONS OF VACANCIES

STARTING SALARY FOR 2023
£Competitive
Plus a great range of rewards and benefits – see website for details.

WORK EXPERIENCE

| INSIGHT COURSES | DEGREE PLACEMENTS | SUMMER INTERNSHIPS |

UNIVERSITY PROMOTIONS DURING 2022-2023
ABERDEEN, ASTON, BIRMINGHAM, BRISTOL, CAMBRIDGE, CARDIFF, CITY, DUNDEE, DURHAM, EDINBURGH, ESSEX, EXETER, GLASGOW, HERIOT-WATT, IMPERIAL COLLEGE LONDON, KING'S COLLEGE LONDON, LEEDS, LEICESTER, LIVERPOOL, LONDON SCHOOL OF ECONOMICS, MANCHESTER, NEWCASTLE, NORTHUMBRIA, NOTTINGHAM, NOTTINGHAM TRENT, OXFORD, PLYMOUTH, QUEEN MARY LONDON, READING, ROYAL HOLLOWAY, SHEFFIELD, SOUTHAMPTON, ST ANDREWS, STRATHCLYDE, SURREY, UEA, UNIVERSITY COLLEGE LONDON, WARWICK

MINIMUM ENTRY REQUIREMENTS
2.1 Degree, 120 UCAS points
Degree in any discipline.
300 UCAS points for those who passed exams before 2017.
Programme dependent and some flex may be shown.
Please see website for details.

APPLICATION DEADLINE
Year-round recruitment
Early application is advised.

FURTHER INFORMATION
www.Top100GraduateEmployers.com
Register now for the latest news, local promotions, work experience and graduate vacancies at KPMG.

Your curiosity can create opportunities

Graduate opportunities 2023 | Nationwide

Audit, Consulting, Deal Advisory, Tax & Law, Technology & Engineering

It's through innovative ideas and robust insights that we make a meaningful difference for the clients and communities we serve. Bring your curiosity, unique perspectives and aspirations to our KPMG community. We'll give you intellectually stimulating opportunities and the support to grow, thrive and make your mark.

Discover more

kpmgcareers.co.uk

kubrick

kubrickgroup.com/join-us

KubrickGroup f joinus@kubrickgroup.com ✉

@KubrickGroup 𝕏 linkedin.com/company/kubrick-group in

@KubrickGroup ⃝ youtube.com/KubrickGroup ▶

GRADUATE VACANCIES IN 2023

CONSULTING

ENGINEERING

TECHNOLOGY

NUMBER OF VACANCIES
900+ graduate jobs

LOCATIONS OF VACANCIES

Vacancies also available in Europe and the USA.

STARTING SALARY FOR 2023
£32,000+

UNIVERSITY PROMOTIONS DURING 2022-2023
ABERDEEN, ABERYSTWYTH, ASTON, BANGOR, BATH, BELFAST, BIRMINGHAM, BRISTOL, CAMBRIDGE, CARDIFF, CITY, DUNDEE, DURHAM, EDINBURGH, ESSEX, EXETER, GLASGOW, HERIOT-WATT, IMPERIAL COLLEGE LONDON, KEELE, KING'S COLLEGE LONDON, KENT, LANCASTER, LEEDS, LEICESTER, LIVERPOOL, LONDON SCHOOL OF ECONOMICS, LOUGHBOROUGH, MANCHESTER, NEWCASTLE, NOTTINGHAM, NOTTINGHAM TRENT, OXFORD, QUEEN MARY LONDON, READING, ROYAL HOLLOWAY, SCHOOL OF AFRICAN STUDIES, SHEFFIELD, SOUTHAMPTON, ST ANDREWS, STIRLING, STRATHCLYDE, SURREY, SUSSEX, SWANSEA, UEA, ULSTER, UNIVERSITY COLLEGE LONDON, WARWICK, YORK
Please check with your university careers service for full details of Kubrick's local promotions and events.

MINIMUM ENTRY REQUIREMENTS
2.1 Degree
All degree subjects accepted.

APPLICATION DEADLINE
Please see website for full details.

FURTHER INFORMATION
www.Top100GraduateEmployers.com
Register now for the latest news, local promotions, work experience and graduate vacancies at Kubrick.

Kubrick was launched in 2016 to overcome the digital skills crisis by giving graduates and junior professionals the chance to enter the data and technology field through bespoke, salaried training and access to real-world client projects. CAGR of circa 260% over 5 years. Kubrick is a UK and US-based organisation.

Kubrick exists to overcome the digital skills crisis by hiring graduates and junior professionals with no technical background and training them over 15 weeks in the latest tools, technologies, and professional skills relevant to their chosen practice area.

Practices span data engineering, data management, data product, machine learning engineering, and cloud engineering, and all degree subjects are welcome. Once trained, consultants are placed with a leading client where they apply their skills to projects over a period of 2 years.

Consultants receive a salary throughout training which increases when they begin their first project, and incrementally increases throughout the 2 years. In addition to salaried training and real-world exposure to projects, consultants can continue developing on site through a bespoke platform and accreditations which are paid for by Kubrick.

They also have access to continuous support from Kubrick throughout their training and client projects plus a wide range of benefits, and can stay connected to their peers and Kubrick employers even if they choose to leave after 2 years, by joining the alumni network.

Kubrick has grown at a rapid rate since launching in 2016 and has since expanded into America to overcome the global digital skills crisis.

To date, they have hired and trained over 1,200 graduates and junior professionals.

Graduate jobs in data, AI, and tech

kubrick

- Instructor led salaried training
- Exposure to real-world projects
- No technical skills required
- Ongoing support
- Continous development

" "

Kubrick were supportive of those who had no prior data experience and wanted a career in data and technology. I don't think there are many companies that offer this as most companies want only those who already have the experience or knowledge-based background.

Sonal Sethi
Data Product Consultant

kubrickgroup.com/join-us

L'ORÉAL

L'Oréal is the world's number one beauty company, with a portfolio of 36 international brands including L'Oréal Paris, Kiehl's, CeraVe, and Garnier, to name a few. L'Oréal's ambition is to become the world's leading beauty tech company, through digital innovation, product, and world-class consumer journeys.

L'Oréal UK & Ireland, the leading player in the multi-billion pound beauty industry in the UK, look for an entrepreneurial mindset in their graduates. They believe in developing their people from the ground up, providing their employees with the opportunity to grow within the company, develop a broad, future focused skill set and build a dynamic career. As a result, a portion of graduate roles are filled by talents from their internship and spring insights programmes, creating a future focused junior talent journey at L'Oréal.

The remainder of the graduates roles are sourced from the external market, to ensure an equal opportunity for all candidates to join this exciting business. On the Management Trainee Programme, they will work in different functions and brands across the business, gaining multiple perspectives of life at L'Oréal.

With three different rotations in their chosen stream, graduates are free to develop their strengths and discover new possibilities, shaping their future career as they go. With development programmes and their own mentor, graduates will progress into operational roles in as little as 18 months. L'Oréal is committed to being one of the top employers in the UK, fostering a workplace where everyone feels welcomed and valued. Promoting gender equality, driving diversity and inclusion, addressing mental health, and establishing evolving workplace practices are a key focus. Through 'L'Oréal for the Future', L'Oréal's global sustainability programme, the business is driving change across all areas including product design, supply chain and consumer behaviour.

GRADUATE VACANCIES IN 2023
ENGINEERING
FINANCE
GENERAL MANAGEMENT
LOGISTICS
MARKETING
SALES

NUMBER OF VACANCIES
35 graduate jobs

LOCATIONS OF VACANCIES

STARTING SALARY FOR 2023
£33,000

WORK EXPERIENCE
INSIGHT COURSES | DEGREE PLACEMENTS | SUMMER INTERNSHIPS

UNIVERSITY PROMOTIONS DURING 2022-2023
ASTON, BATH, BIRMINGHAM, BRISTOL, CAMBRIDGE, CARDIFF, DURHAM, EDINBURGH, EXETER, GLASGOW, IMPERIAL COLLEGE LONDON, LANCASTER, LEEDS, LONDON SCHOOL OF ECONOMICS, LOUGHBOROUGH, MANCHESTER, NEWCASTLE, NOTTINGHAM, NOTTINGHAM TRENT, OXFORD, ST ANDREWS, SURREY, SUSSEX, ULSTER, UNIVERSITY COLLEGE LONDON, WARWICK
Please check with your university careers service for full details of L'Oréal's local promotions and events.

MINIMUM ENTRY REQUIREMENTS
Any degree accepted

APPLICATION DEADLINE
January 2023

FURTHER INFORMATION
www.Top100GraduateEmployers.com
Register now for the latest news, local promotions, work experience and graduate vacancies at L'Oréal.

FREEDOM TO GO BEYOND, THAT'S THE BEAUTY OF L'ORÉAL.

Our brands, dynamic culture, and a mindset of always being our own challenger, mean that we offer autonomy and opportunities you won't get anywhere else.

At L'Oréal UK and Ireland you are trusted to succeed.

Graduate and Internship opportunities at:
CAREERS.LOREAL.COM

LATHAM&WATKINS LLP

Latham & Watkins is one of the world's largest law firms, with more than 3,000 attorneys in offices across Europe, the US, the Middle East, and Asia. The firm is a global leader in corporate transactions, environmental law, finance matters, litigations and trials, and tax services.

Latham & Watkins' non-hierarchical, collegiate management style and ambitious and entrepreneurial culture make it a unique place to work. Over 70% of the firm's transactions involve five or more offices, and the collaborative atmosphere is strengthened by the firm's diversity. Latham's global diversity strategy and initiatives work to strengthen and promote the firm as a workplace where the best and brightest attorneys from all groups excel and find the opportunities and support to fulfil their potential to become firm and industry leaders.

The firm offers exceptional training and support to ensure seamless collaboration on projects that span time zones, teams, and offices in the world's major financial, business, and regulatory centres. Latham is known for advising some of the world's leading corporates, financial institutions, and private equity firms on market-shaping transactions, disputes, and regulatory matters.

Pro bono is a cornerstone of Latham's culture. Since 2000, Latham has provided almost 4 million pro bono hours in free legal services to underserved individuals and families and the non-profit sector, valued at more than US$2 billion.

Latham offers a training contract with real responsibility, combined with supervision from market-leading lawyers on complex, high-profile, and cross-border work. The firm looks for outstanding people who have the potential to become exceptional lawyers. Initiative, communication skills, complex thinking, willingness to assume responsibility, resilience, and judgement are some of the traits particularly valued at Latham.

GRADUATE VACANCIES IN 2023

LAW

NUMBER OF VACANCIES
32 graduate jobs
For training contracts starting in 2025.

LOCATIONS OF VACANCIES

STARTING SALARY FOR 2023
£50,000

WORK EXPERIENCE
INSIGHT COURSES | SUMMER INTERNSHIPS

UNIVERSITY PROMOTIONS DURING 2023-2023
BIRMINGHAM, BRISTOL, CAMBRIDGE, CARDIFF, DURHAM, EDINBURGH, EXETER, GLASGOW, KING'S COLLEGE LONDON, LEEDS, LONDON SCHOOL OF ECONOMICS, MANCHESTER, NOTTINGHAM, OXFORD, QUEEN MARY LONDON, ST ANDREWS, UNIVERSITY COLLEGE LONDON, WARWICK, YORK
Please check with your university careers service for full details of Latham & Watkins' local promotions and events.

MINIMUM ENTRY REQUIREMENTS
2.1 Degree

APPLICATION DEADLINE
Varies by function

FURTHER INFORMATION
www.Top100GraduateEmployers.com
Register now for the latest news, local promotions, work experience and graduate vacancies at Latham & Watkins.

WHEN YOU JOIN LATHAM & WATKINS

There's no limit to what you can achieve

It won't be long before you're working on your own transactions and cases, instead of reading up on existing ones.

At Latham & Watkins, you'll get the chance to make a big impact in small teams. And you'll be surrounded by experts who are invested in seeing you succeed.

Discover the opportunities

LATHAM & WATKINS

lidlgraduatecareers.co.uk

linkedin.com/company/company/lidl-gb **in**

youtube.com/LidlUKOfficial ▶

Lidl. The game-changing supermarket known for being big on quality, Lidl on price. 920+ stores. 13 Warehouses. And over 28,000 colleagues nationwide. This is one of the UK's fastest growing retailers, and with this comes exciting opportunities for graduates to make their mark on the business.

From being committed to sustainability, to working with local charities and food redistributors through various CSR programmes – Lidl are more than just a discount retailer. Lidl are looking for ambitious, dedicated talent with personality and potential to join their graduate programmes; to challenge and change the world of grocery retail, and to become one of Lidl's future leaders.

Lidl's structured graduate programmes take early careers to the next level. Designed with rapid development in mind, graduates will be provided with all of the tools they need to succeed. And with their commitment to building at least 50 new stores and one Regional Distribution Centre every year, there will be plenty of opportunity for graduates to develop, progress, and really make a mark on the business.

Graduates will learn from the best in the business, with each programme uniquely tailored to provide hands on, structured training, providing a clear development path in one of Lidl's core business areas. Lidl are also expanding their range of Head Office graduate programmes, based in their brand new, state of the art Head Office in Tolworth, South West London.

From day one, graduates will build skills and realise their potential as they find out what it takes to be part of something big, as they play their part in feeding the nation. With great pay and brilliant benefits, including 30 days' holiday per year, an in-store discount, and extra discounts on gym memberships, cinema tickets and much more, there's never been a better time to join Lidl GB.

GRADUATE VACANCIES IN 2023

GENERAL MANAGEMENT

LOGISTICS

MARKETING

PROPERTY

PURCHASING

RETAIL

SALES

NUMBER OF VACANCIES
90+ graduate jobs

LOCATIONS OF VACANCIES

STARTING SALARY FOR 2023
£37,000

WORK EXPERIENCE
DEGREE
PLACEMENTS

UNIVERSITY PROMOTIONS DURING 2022-2023
Please check with your university careers service for full details of Lidl's local promotions and events.

MINIMUM ENTRY REQUIREMENTS
2.2 Degree

APPLICATION DEADLINE
Varies by function

FURTHER INFORMATION
www.Top100GraduateEmployers.com
Register now for the latest news, local promotions, work experience and graduate vacancies at Lidl.

Big on ambition.
Even bigger on opportunities.

If you've got the drive, we've got the journey. Build skills and confidence on our graduate programmes and discover what it takes to be part of something great. An operation that feeds the nation.

A career a lidl less ordinary.

🔍 lidlcareers.co.uk

LinklatersGradsUK trainee.recruitment@linklaters.com ✉

@LinklatersGrads ✖ linkedin.com/company/linklaters in

@linklatersgraduatesuk ⬡ youtube.com/LinklatersCareers ▶

Linklaters

From a shifting geopolitical landscape to the exponential growth in FinTech, this is a time of unprecedented change. Linklaters is ready. They go further to support clients, with market-leading legal insight and innovation. And they go further for each other, too.

When people join Linklaters, they find colleagues they want to work with. Inspiring, personable professionals who are generous with their time and always happy to help. Because to be best in class, Linklaters looks for open-minded, team-spirited individuals who will collaborate – and innovate – to deliver the smartest solutions for clients.

Linklaters recruits candidates from a range of different backgrounds and disciplines, not just law. Why? Because those candidates bring with them a set of unique skills and perspectives that can help to challenge conventional thinking and inspire different approaches to client problems.

All Linklaters trainees benefit from pioneering learning and development opportunities, and an inclusive working culture that encourages them to fulfil their potential.

Over two years, trainees take four six-month seats (placements) in different practice areas and sometimes abroad. They work on high-profile deals across a global network of 30 offices, and gain the knowledge they need to qualify. And, throughout their career, they enjoy the advantage of world-class training, courtesy of the Linklaters Learning & Development team.

With their uniquely future-focused culture and high-profile, global opportunities, Linklaters provides the ideal preparation for a rewarding career, no matter what the future holds.

Great change is here. Get ready.

GRADUATE VACANCIES IN 2023
LAW

NUMBER OF VACANCIES
100 graduate jobs
For training contracts starting in 2025.

LOCATIONS OF VACANCIES

STARTING SALARY FOR 2023
£50,000

WORK EXPERIENCE
INSIGHT COURSES SUMMER INTERNSHIPS

UNIVERSITY PROMOTIONS DURING 2021-2022
BELFAST, BIRMINGHAM, BRISTOL, CAMBRIDGE, CARDIFF, CITY, DURHAM, EDINBURGH, ESSEX, EXETER, GLASGOW, IMPERIAL COLLEGE LONDON, KING'S COLLEGE LONDON, KENT, LANCASTER, LEEDS, LEICESTER, LSE, MANCHESTER, NOTTINGHAM, NOTTINGHAM TRENT, OXFORD, OXFORD BROOKES, QUEEN MARY LONDON, SCHOOL OF AFRICAN STUDIES, SHEFFIELD, SOUTHAMPTON, ST ANDREWS, SURREY, SUSSEX, SWANSEA, UEA, UNIVERSITY COLLEGE LONDON, WARWICK, YORK
Please check with your university careers service for full details of Linklaters' local promotions and events.

MINIMUM ENTRY REQUIREMENTS
2.1 Degree

APPLICATION DEADLINE
15th December 2022

FURTHER INFORMATION
www.Top100GraduateEmployers.com
Register now for the latest news, local promotions, work experience and graduate vacancies at Linklaters.

Great change is here.
Linklaters

Are you ready?

From a shifting geopolitical landscape
to the exponential growth in FinTech,
this is a time of unprecedented change.

At Linklaters, we're ready. Our people
go further to support our clients,
with market-leading legal insight and
innovation. And we go further for each
other, too. We're people you want to work
with, generous with our time and ready
to help. So no matter what the future
holds, with us you'll be one step ahead.
Great change is here. Get ready.

Find out more at careers.linklaters.com

With over 26 million customers, Lloyds Banking Group is the largest UK retail and commercial financial services provider. It offers a wide range of opportunities to make a real impact on customers, communities, and the planet, through brands like Lloyds Bank, Halifax, Bank of Scotland and Scottish Widows.

The world is constantly evolving. New knowledge and technologies are impacting how people bank every day. To meet the ever-changing needs of their customers, Lloyds Banking Group is welcoming a new digital future. They're inviting graduates with a wide range of skills and experience to explore the possibilities of this transformation with them.

The Group is looking for graduates who are excited by rewarding challenges, who want to be part of its commitment to long-term sustainability, and who are inspired by the purpose of Helping Britain Prosper. Whether it's forming relationships with clients or developing the next generation of technology, graduates will have a real impact on the journey Lloyds Banking Group is taking.

There are a variety of graduate opportunities available – from Software Engineering to Data Science, Finance to Risk, Sustainable Financial Wellbeing and more. Whichever area graduates choose, they'll get support to achieve professional qualifications as well as long-term career progression and development.

Best of all, they'll grow in a genuinely inclusive and supportive environment, where learning is central, flexible working is championed, and everyone is free to be themselves. Because Lloyds Banking Group understands people do their best work when they feel valued, respected and trusted.

Imagine what's next, for graduates and the future of financial services, at Lloyds Banking Group.

GRADUATE VACANCIES IN 2023

ACCOUNTANCY
ENGINEERING
FINANCE
HUMAN RESOURCES
INVESTMENT BANKING
TECHNOLOGY

NUMBER OF VACANCIES
100+ graduate jobs

LOCATIONS OF VACANCIES

STARTING SALARY FOR 2023
£31,000
Plus a discretionary bonus, a settling-in allowance, and flexible working.

WORK EXPERIENCE

INSIGHT COURSES | DEGREE PLACEMENTS | SUMMER INTERNSHIPS

UNIVERSITY PROMOTIONS DURING 2022-2023
ASTON, BATH, BIRMINGHAM, BRISTOL, CAMBRIDGE, CARDIFF, DUNDEE, DURHAM, EDINBURGH, GLASGOW, IMPERIAL COLLEGE LONDON, KING'S COLLEGE LONDON, LANCASTER, LEEDS, LEICESTER, LIVERPOOL, LONDON SCHOOL OF ECONOMICS, MANCHESTER, NEWCASTLE, NOTTINGHAM, OXFORD, QUEEN MARY LONDON, SHEFFIELD, ST ANDREWS, STRATHCLYDE, UEA, UNIVERSITY COLLEGE LONDON, WARWICK, YORK

MINIMUM ENTRY REQUIREMENTS
2.2 Degree

APPLICATION DEADLINE
Varies by function

FURTHER INFORMATION
www.Top100GraduateEmployers.com
*Register now for the latest news, local promotions, work experience and graduate vacancies at **Lloyds Banking Group**.*

CODING CAPABILITIES. PERFECTED.

Imagine the future of financial services. Imagine how technology can keep changing the way people bank. Imagine how it can become greener, more sustainable. How it can Help Britain Prosper. Imagine being part of making that happen.

People like Rose don't have to. As one of our software engineering graduates her work is already making a difference to our business and its 26 million customers. And as she's helping us grow, we're helping her do the same. From learning how to programme from scratch to feeling comfortable asking for help, she's developing as a person, as well as an engineer, every day.

If you want a future that promises progression as well as unlimited ways to help our business, customers and communities prosper, come and explore the possibilities with us.

What's next for your career?
Head to lloydsbankinggrouptalent.com to find out.

Imagine what's next

MARS

GRADUATE VACANCIES IN 2023

ENGINEERING
FINANCE
GENERAL MANAGEMENT
MARKETING
RESEARCH & DEVELOPMENT
SALES
TECHNOLOGY

NUMBER OF VACANCIES
25 graduate jobs

LOCATIONS OF VACANCIES

Vacancies also available in Europe.

STARTING SALARY FOR 2023
£32,000
Plus a £2,000 starting bonus and annual company bonus.

UNIVERSITY PROMOTIONS DURING 2022-2023
ASTON, BATH, BIRMINGHAM, CAMBRIDGE, DURHAM, EXETER, LEEDS, NOTTINGHAM, OXFORD, UNIVERSITY COLLEGE LONDON
Please check with your university careers service for full details of Mars' local promotions and events.

MINIMUM ENTRY REQUIREMENTS
2.1 Degree;
Varies by function
Relevant degree required for some roles.

APPLICATION DEADLINE
Varies by function

FURTHER INFORMATION
www.Top100GraduateEmployers.com
Register now for the latest news, local promotions, work experience and graduate vacancies at Mars.

For generations, families across the world – including the four-legged members – have loved Mars brands, products, and services. Mars is 130,000 Associates across 80 countries, working hard to create the world's most loved products, including M&M'S®, EXTRA®, PEDIGREE®, WHISKAS®, and Dolmio®.

Mars might be a global business, but it's more like a community than a corporate – it's still a private, family-owned business built up of a family of Associates. Associates at Mars are united and guided by The Five Principles – Quality, Responsibility, Mutuality, Efficiency, and Freedom; these are key to the culture and help Associates make decisions they are proud of.

The culture at Mars is relationship-driven – and it's how these relationships are built that's most important. Collaborating with others is key. Mars encourages open communication, as this builds relationships formed of trust and respect.

Mars wants to stretch and challenge Associates every day to help them reach their full potential. So, they take learning and development seriously – it makes good business sense for Mars to have people performing at the top of their game. With great line managers, mentors, coaches and peers, graduates will be supported the whole way. And they will support other Associates to learn and grow on their journey too.

At Mars, graduates are offered an unrivalled opportunity from day one. Mars wants everything they do to matter – from the smallest things to the largest – and Mars wants their work to make a positive impact on the world around them. Graduates will have endless support to develop both personally and professionally, creating a start today, to an exciting and rewarding career tomorrow.

Start your tomorrow, today, with Mars.

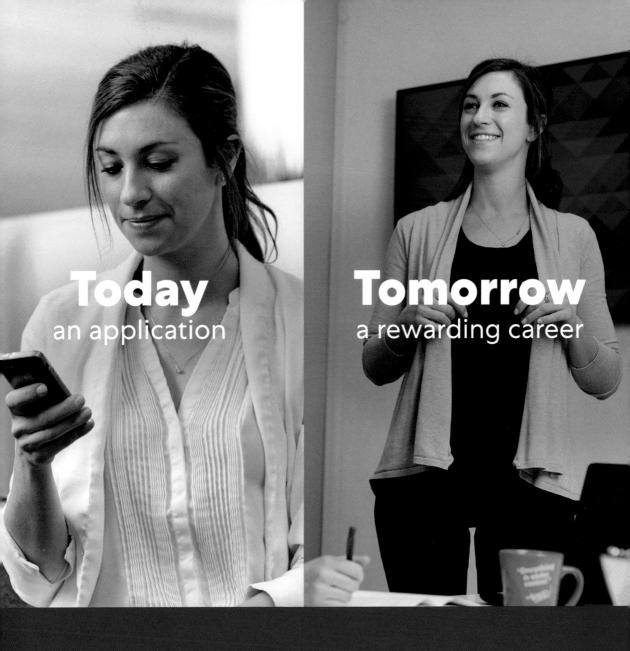

Today
an application

Tomorrow
a rewarding career

At Mars, the choices you make today shape the opportunities you get tomorrow. So whether you want to live and work in another country, have the freedom to move your career in any direction, or work on projects that make a difference to our world – you have the power to make it happen. Join one of our Graduate Leadership Experiences and get the support you need to start a brilliant career.

Visit **careers.mars.com/Students-Graduates**

#TomorrowStartsToday

MARS   Your tomorrow starts today

SECURITYSERVICE
MI5

MI5 helps safeguard the UK against threats to national security including terrorism and espionage. It investigates suspect individuals and organisations to gather intelligence relating to security threats. MI5 also advises the critical national infrastructure on protective security measures.

MI5 is a friendly, inclusive organisation which values diversity of background and diversity of thought. Graduates who join MI5 can expect stimulating and rewarding careers in a supportive environment, whilst enjoying a good work-life balance.

Many graduates join the Intelligence Officer Development Programme, which is a structured four-year programme designed to teach new joiners about MI5 investigations and to give them the skills to run them.

MI5 also deals with vast amounts of data, and interpreting that data is vital to its intelligence work. The Intelligence and Data Analyst Development Programme is a structured five-year programme which prepares individuals with potential to be part of this specialist career stream.

MI5 also offers a structured Technology Graduate Development Programme, which gives graduates the experience, knowledge, and skills they need to be an effective technology professional in the organisation's pioneering IT function.

Graduates who are looking for a rewarding career in corporate services can join MI5 as Business Enablers, where they can develop a breadth of experience undertaking corporate roles across a range of business areas, before having the opportunity to specialise in a particular area.

Graduates can also join as Russian or Mandarin analysts, working at the core of MI5's operational teams and using their language skills to provide intelligence insights.

GRADUATE VACANCIES IN 2023

FINANCE
GENERAL MANAGEMENT
HUMAN RESOURCES
INTELLIGENCE GATHERING
TECHNOLOGY

NUMBER OF VACANCIES
200+ graduate jobs

LOCATIONS OF VACANCIES

STARTING SALARY FOR 2022
£33,350+

WORK EXPERIENCE

INSIGHT COURSES | DEGREE PLACEMENTS | SUMMER INTERNSHIPS

UNIVERSITY PROMOTIONS DURING 2022-2023
Please check with your university careers service for full details of MI5's local promotions and events.

MINIMUM ENTRY REQUIREMENTS
2.2 Degree
Or relevant work experience.

APPLICATION DEADLINE
Varies by function

FURTHER INFORMATION
www.Top100GraduateEmployers.com
Register now for the latest news, local promotions, work experience and graduate vacancies at MI5.

Combine exciting opportunities

with fascinating work

to keep the country safe

Technology is rapidly evolving and it's vital for MI5 to stay one step ahead. That is why we need graduates with a passion for technology who can come up with innovative solutions to a wide range of technological challenges. MI5 offers varied and rewarding careers in a supportive and encouraging environment that puts the emphasis on teamwork. Whichever path you choose you will be working with technology to help keep the country safe.

Discover your role at www.mi5.gov.uk/careers

Morgan Stanley

morganstanley.com/campus

MorganStanley **f**

@MorganStanley **y**   linkedin.com/company/morgan-stanley **in**

@Morgan.Stanley **O**   youtube.com/MorganStanley **▶**

WE ARE
Morgan Stanley

Morgan Stanley is one of the world's leading financial services firms. It generates, manages, and distributes capital, helping businesses get the funds they need to develop innovative products and services that benefit millions. Its work is defined by the passion and dedication of its people.

Morgan Stanley is committed to maintaining the first-class service and high standard of excellence that has always defined the firm. At its foundation are five core values – putting clients first, doing the right thing, leading with exceptional ideas, committing to diversity and inclusion, and giving back – that guides its more than 70,000 employees in 1,200 offices across 41 countries.

At Morgan Stanley, attitude is just as important as aptitude, and it seeks to work with and develop students and graduates who show integrity and commitment to the firm's core values; who share its commitment to providing first-class client service, and who embrace change and innovation. Because the firm values a diversity of perspectives, it encourages people to be themselves and to pursue personal interests. This is why Morgan Stanley accepts applicants from all degree disciplines who are eager to learn and contribute.

Morgan Stanley's goals are achieved through hiring, training, and promoting the best possible talent. There are numerous opportunities to learn, grow professionally, and help put the power of capital to work. Morgan Stanley's programmes are designed to provide the knowledge and skills graduates can apply to develop quickly into successful professionals in their chosen area.

Training is not limited to the first weeks or months on the job, but continues throughout a graduate's career. Over time, they could become part of the next generation of leaders, playing a part in technological, banking and cultural advancements that change the world forever.

GRADUATE VACANCIES IN 2023

ACCOUNTANCY

ENGINEERING

FINANCE

HUMAN RESOURCES

INVESTMENT BANKING

LAW

MARKETING

RESEARCH AND DEVELOPMENT

SALES

TECHNOLOGY

NUMBER OF VACANCIES
300+ graduate jobs

LOCATIONS OF VACANCIES

STARTING SALARY FOR 2023
£Competitive

WORK EXPERIENCE

| INSIGHT COURSES | DEGREE PLACEMENTS | SUMMER INTERNSHIPS |

UNIVERSITY PROMOTIONS DURING 2022-2023
Please check with your university careers service for full details of Morgan Stanley's local promotions and events.

MINIMUM ENTRY REQUIREMENTS
2.1 Degree

APPLICATION DEADLINE
Varies by function
Early application is advised

FURTHER INFORMATION
www.Top100GraduateEmployers.com
Register now for the latest news, local promotions, work experience and graduate vacancies at Morgan Stanley.

WE ARE IN SEARCH OF GREAT MINDS THAT THINK NOTHING ALIKE.

We believe our greatest asset is our people. We value our commitment to diverse perspectives and a culture of inclusion across the firm.

A career at Morgan Stanley means belonging to an ideas-driven culture that embraces new perspectives to solve complex problems.

Discover who we are.
morganstanley.com/campus

WE ARE
Morgan Stanley

Mariam
Bank Resource Management

Mott MacDonald is a global engineering, management, and development consultancy focused on guiding clients through many of the planet's most intricate challenges. By challenging norms and unlocking creativity, Mott MacDonald delivers long-lasting value for societies around the globe.

Mott MacDonald's purpose is to improve society by considering social outcomes in all they do, relentlessly focusing on excellence and digital innovation, transforming clients' businesses, their communities, and employee opportunities. Their 16,000-strong network of experts are joined up across sectors and geographies, giving their graduates access to an exceptional breadth of expertise and experience, enhancing their knowledge with the right support and guidance every step of the way.

The consultancy's employees – active in 150 countries – take leading roles on some of the world's highest profile projects, turning obstacles into elegant, sustainable solutions. Individuals who get satisfaction from working on projects that benefit communities around the world will thrive at Mott MacDonald.

Additionally, as Mott MacDonald is an employee-owned company, it allows them to choose the work they take on and focus on the issues that are important.

Mott MacDonald's graduate schemes are more than just graduate jobs. With the help of a dedicated learning and development team, the accredited schemes aim to give graduates the opportunity to continually progress and develop in their chosen field.

All entry-level professionals are enrolled in Accelerating Your Future, a structured development programme that introduces key business and commercial competencies, enabling graduates to be the best that they can be.

GRADUATE VACANCIES IN 2023
CONSULTING
ENGINEERING
PROPERTY
TECHNOLOGY

NUMBER OF VACANCIES
400 graduate jobs

LOCATIONS OF VACANCIES

STARTING SALARY FOR 2023
£27,500-£31,000
Plus relocation allowance.

WORK EXPERIENCE
DEGREE PLACEMENTS | SUMMER INTERNSHIPS

UNIVERSITY PROMOTIONS DURING 2022-2023
BIRMINGHAM, BRISTOL, CAMBRIDGE, CARDIFF, DURHAM, EDINBURGH, GLASGOW, HERIOT-WATT, IMPERIAL COLLEGE LONDON, LANCASTER, LEEDS, LIVERPOOL, LOUGHBOROUGH, MANCHESTER, NEWCASTLE, NORTHUMBRIA, NOTTINGHAM, READING, SHEFFIELD, SOUTHAMPTON, STRATHCLYDE, UNIVERSITY COLLEGE LONDON, WARWICK
Please check with your university careers service for full details of Mott MacDonald's local promotions and events.

MINIMUM ENTRY REQUIREMENTS
Varies by function
Relevant degree required for some roles.

APPLICATION DEADLINE
November 2022

FURTHER INFORMATION
www.Top100GraduateEmployers.com
Register now for the latest news, local promotions, work experience and graduate vacancies at Mott MacDonald.

NatWest Group

 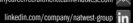

NatWest Group are guided by their purpose to champion potential, helping people, families and businesses to thrive. They know that when their customers and communities succeed they do too. This purpose enables them to build long term value, sustainable growth and make a positive contribution to society.

NatWest Group are committed to making this purpose work for all. Graduate, intern, and insight programmes at NatWest Group offer structured and supported learning with pathways allowing students and graduates to join the part of the bank that suits them best. They help colleagues to thrive by promising a fulfilling role, fair pay, excellent training, and great leadership.

Focusing on things they believe everyone shares – the need for financial security, the desire to improve a person's place in society, and the environment everyone lives in – NatWest Group aims to empower individuals and communities wherever they are.

They use their expertise to share knowledge and skills which help people improve their financial wellbeing, through initiatives such as their long-standing MoneySense programme. They open doors to business and encourage entrepreneurship, particularly among underrepresented groups. And they're a major funder of renewable energy projects, while driving their own operations to be carbon positive.

A career here means benefiting from an inclusive culture where individual strengths and working styles are appreciated and encouraged. And because of their significant investment in technology, no matter where people or their colleagues are based, working at NatWest Group is more flexible than it's ever been. Graduates and Interns collaborate across the organisation; getting the support they need to make a positive difference with the work they do.

GRADUATE VACANCIES IN 2023

CONSULTING
FINANCE
HUMAN RESOURCES
TECHNOLOGY

NUMBER OF VACANCIES
400+ graduate jobs

LOCATIONS OF VACANCIES

STARTING SALARY FOR 2023
£33,500-£60,000

WORK EXPERIENCE

| INSIGHT COURSES | DEGREE PLACEMENTS | SUMMER INTERNSHIPS |

UNIVERSITY PROMOTIONS DURING 2022-2023
ASTON, BELFAST, BIRMINGHAM, CITY, DUNDEE, EDINBURGH, GLASGOW, HERIOT-WATT, IMPERIAL COLLEGE LONDON, KING'S COLLEGE LONDON, LANCASTER, LEEDS, LEICESTER, LIVERPOOL, LONDON SCHOOL OF ECONOMICS, MANCHESTER, NOTTINGHAM, QUEEN MARY LONDON, STRATHCLYDE, ULSTER, UNIVERSITY COLLEGE LONDON, WARWICK
Please check with your university careers service for full details of NatWest's local promotions and events.

MINIMUM ENTRY REQUIREMENTS
2.1 Degree

APPLICATION DEADLINE
Year-round recruitment
Early application is advised.

FURTHER INFORMATION
www.Top100GraduateEmployers.com
Register now for the latest news, local promotions, work experience and graduate vacancies at NatWest.

Hey you!

NatWest Group

Whoever you are, whatever your story - if you're bright and ambitious and want to help others thrive - check out jobs.natwestgroup.com today.

Our graduate and intern programmes are an exciting opportunity for you to help us build long-lasting relationships with our customers that contribute to their success. Because when our customers succeed, we succeed. And you do too.

Find your perfect role at NatWest, where you can be yourself, enjoy a healthy work-life balance and find your moment to step up and shine.

NEWTON

workatnewton.com

graduates@newtoneurope.com

linkedin.com/company/newton-europe-limited

NewtonEurope f   @NewtonEurope o   youtube.com/NewtonEuropeLtd

GRADUATE VACANCIES IN 2023
CONSULTING

NUMBER OF VACANCIES
155-165 graduate jobs

LOCATIONS OF VACANCIES

STARTING SALARY FOR 2023
£45,000-£50,000 package
Inclusive of bi-annual profit share bonus, matched pension contribution and car options. Plus a sign-on bonus of up to £5,500.

WORK EXPERIENCE
SUMMER INTERNSHIPS

UNIVERSITY PROMOTIONS DURING 2022-2023
BATH, BIRMINGHAM, BRISTOL, CAMBRIDGE, DURHAM, EDINBURGH, EXETER, IMPERIAL COLLEGE LONDON, LONDON SCHOOL OF ECONOMICS, MANCHESTER, NOTTINGHAM, OXFORD, STRATHCLYDE, UNIVERSITY COLLEGE LONDON, WARWICK
Please check with your university careers service for full details of Newton's local promotions and events.

MINIMUM ENTRY REQUIREMENTS
Any degree accepted

APPLICATION DEADLINE
February 2023

FURTHER INFORMATION
www.Top100GraduateEmployers.com
*Register now for the latest news, local promotions, work experience and graduate vacancies at **Newton**.*

Newton is a business consultancy focused on operational improvement. An organisation that's vastly different from other players in the same industry, Newton's people are driven by a fundamental belief that even the best organisations can be better.

The difference Newton brings begins with the way they approach consulting. They work hand in hand with clients, getting to the heart of the issue. This means they are not about compiling reports; rather, it's about delivering what's in those reports. Doing the work – creating an impact. It's the best way to crack some of the largest and most complex challenges that our country faces.

Newton is filled with some of the sharpest as well as the nicest people in the industry – the sort of people who pursue brave ideas and believe everything can be better. The enthusiasm, curiosity, tenacity and ease of communication are infectious and distinctly set the firm apart. Graduates play a big part in bringing in new perspectives, energy and potential to this thriving firm.

They are steadfast in their belief that organisations don't solve problems, people do, and this has empowered them to shape a unique culture that's all about fun, friendship and high performance. The organisation is so confident about the way they work, and their ability to deliver results that they guarantee their fees against the impact they make.

Measurable results that significantly change the way their clients operate. For instance, working with a County Council's Children Services department, they helped reduce the number of children going into residential care from 40 per year to 17. Newton brings together committed people who are driven to make a lasting change in an open and inclusive environment. It inspires everyone, helps them learn and grow together and do more from day one.

ACTIONS SPEAK LOUDER THAN 20,000 WORDS.

To solve our clients' challenges, we go beyond compiling reports. We work side-by-side with the client. Understanding their process and the challenges they face. Analysing the data, approaching the problem from different perspectives. Most importantly, delivering results that matter. Implementing the solution to leave behind a lasting impact. Since 2001, we've brought real and sustainable operational change to a number of industries. By changing the way consulting works. At Newton, it's what we do every day. Together, let's make a greater impact. Let's start doing.

To find out if a career in consulting is right for you, search **Newton Graduate Careers or visit WorkatNewton.com**

Thea, Digital Consultant

The NGDP is a two-year programme which gives graduates the opportunity and training to fast-track their career in local government. Local government is responsible for providing over 800 vital community services, and employs more than one million people to deliver them.

The NGDP exists to find and support the next generation of sector leadership. It welcomes graduates motivated by a desire to lead in the public sector, whether they are driven by a specific issue or more broadly want their work to have a positive, tangible impact. Now in it's 20th year, the NGDP has brought nearly 2,000 graduates into local government.

NGDP graduate trainees make a real contribution to shaping and implementing new ideas and initiatives from their first day. Each trainee is employed by a participating council for two years, during which time they rotate between a minimum of three different placements across key areas of the council. In the last two years, NGDP trainees have pioneered digital inclusion projects, refreshed their council's diversity and inclusion strategy, led climate emergency initiatives and have played a key role in public health initiatives. These are just a few examples of the placements in which NGDP trainees gain valuable knowledge, experience, and transferable skills, all of which make them highly sought after in the public sector workforce.

The NGDP expects to recruit a cohort of at least 150 trainees next year, placing each individual into a supportive community of peers. Councils provide placement coordinators and mentors for trainees, while the scheme's learning programme develops trainees' management skills and deepens their knowledge of the sector. Completion of the programme earns graduates a top-level Institute for Leadership and Management qualification.

GRADUATE VACANCIES IN 2023
GENERAL MANAGEMENT

NUMBER OF VACANCIES
150+ graduate jobs

LOCATIONS OF VACANCIES

STARTING SALARY FOR 2023
£26,446+

UNIVERSITY PROMOTIONS DURING 2022-2023
ASTON, BATH, BIRMINGHAM, BRADFORD, BRISTOL, CITY, ESSEX, KING'S COLLEGE LONDON, LANCASTER, LEEDS, LEICESTER, LIVERPOOL, LONDON SCHOOL OF ECONOMICS, LOUGHBOROUGH, MANCHESTER, NEWCASTLE, NOTTINGHAM, NOTTINGHAM TRENT, OXFORD BROOKES, QUEEN MARY LONDON, READING, ROYAL HOLLOWAY, SCHOOL OF AFRICAN STUDIES, SHEFFIELD, SOUTHAMPTON, SURREY, SUSSEX, UEA, UNIVERSITY COLLEGE LONDON, WARWICK, YORK
Please check with your university careers service for full details of the NGDP's local promotions and events.

MINIMUM ENTRY REQUIREMENTS
2.2 Degree

APPLICATION DEADLINE
January 2023

FURTHER INFORMATION
www.Top100GraduateEmployers.com
Register now for the latest news, local promotions, work experience and graduate vacancies at the NGDP.

Graduate Management Training Scheme

The National Health Service (NHS) is Europe's largest employer, with an annual budget of over £130 billion and a mission to improve the wellbeing of 57 million people. Its Graduate Management Training Scheme (GMTS) is a great place to begin a journey towards becoming a healthcare leader of the future.

GMTS trainees specialise in one of six areas: General Management, Human Resources, Finance, Policy & Strategy, Health Informatics or Health Analysis. Their work can be in hospital or office settings, and can range from A&E data analysis to service improvement to financial planning and much more.

Trainees get access to a comprehensive development package, including on-the-job training on placements where they gain specialist skills, and post-graduate qualifications from leading universities. On-scheme support includes pastoral and placement managers and a trainee buddy. And with 250 graduates joining GMTS in 2023, there are opportunities to build far-reaching networks with other trainees.

The Scheme has won multiple awards and gives endless ways to grow personally and professionally while taking early leadership responsibility. Graduates are selected based on their leadership potential and ambition to make a difference through a management career in healthcare.

The NHS offers both great responsibility and potential. On this fast track to senior leadership, graduates quickly face the exhilarating challenge of handling complex problems and high-profile situations. Which means future NHS leaders need the resilience, tenacity and focus to achieve the best results. Ultimately, it's an incredibly rewarding path where hard work and commitment can affect the lives of millions – and be completely life-changing for graduates themselves – in an organisation like no other in the world.

GRADUATE VACANCIES IN 2023
ACCOUNTANCY
FINANCE
GENERAL MANAGEMENT
HUMAN RESOURCES
TECHNOLOGY

NUMBER OF VACANCIES
250 graduate jobs

LOCATIONS OF VACANCIES

STARTING SALARY FOR 2023
£25,368
Based on 2022 salary. Check website for latest salary & benefit information.

UNIVERSITY PROMOTIONS DURING 2022-2023
ASTON, BATH, BIRMINGHAM, BRADFORD, BRISTOL, BRUNEL, CAMBRIDGE, CARDIFF, CITY, DURHAM, ESSEX, EXETER, IMPERIAL COLLEGE LONDON, KING'S COLLEGE LONDON, KENT, LANCASTER, LEEDS, LEICESTER, LIVERPOOL, LOUGHBOROUGH, MANCHESTER, NEWCASTLE, NORTHUMBRIA, NOTTINGHAM, NOTTINGHAM TRENT, OXFORD, PLYMOUTH, READING, SHEFFIELD, SOUTHAMPTON, SURREY, SUSSEX, SWANSEA, UEA, UNIVERSITY COLLEGE LONDON, WARWICK, YORK
Please check with your university careers service for full details of the NHS's local promotions and events.

MINIMUM ENTRY REQUIREMENTS
2.2 Degree
Degree with numerate content required for Health Analysis roles.

APPLICATION DEADLINE
31st October 2022

FURTHER INFORMATION
www.Top100GraduateEmployers.com
Register now for the latest news, local promotions, work experience and graduate vacancies at the NHS.

**Graduate Management
Training Scheme**

It's not who you are.
It's what you will become.

**The NHS Graduate Management Training Scheme (GMTS)
offers you a fast track to becoming a non-clinical senior
leader. In an organisation that can positively impact 57
million people and begin a life-changing journey for you.**

It's not your degree subject or the type of person you are that matters.
It's your leadership potential.

Whichever GMTS specialism you join, it's about your potential to face
challenges head on. To inspire and effect change.

It's about your potential to become a respected healthcare leader who
helps shape the future of the NHS. And, potentially, the lives of millions.

Start your journey here

www.graduates.nhs.uk

P&G

P&G is one of the world's largest consumer goods companies, with employees from over 140 countries, and operations in approximately 70 countries. P&G aspires to build a better world – with equal voice and equal representation for everyone, and by being a leader in environmental sustainability.

A graduate role at P&G means starting a real job with real responsibility, straight out of university. Whether new joiners are students, graduates, or experienced professionals, they won't experience any rotational programmes or gradual onboarding here. Instead, from Day 1, they'll be able to dive into the meaningful work that makes an impact on P&G's leading brands, the world, and their careers. P&G invests heavily into the early development of their talents as they promote from within their own ranks, continuously aiming to grow the skills of their employees.

P&G offers a creative and dynamic work environment where their employees are at the core of everything they do. Whether helping to design their latest front-end innovation, selling to some of the UK and Ireland's biggest retailers, or designing a full-blown product launch, P&G employees will be empowered to succeed.

Most of all, P&G strives to represent the diversity of the consumers they serve. With around 60 nationalities represented in their Northern Europe workforce, their own diversity helps them to understand and meet the varied needs of consumers around the world.

All of which enables them to constantly challenge the status quo! From redesigning products (e.g. H&S beach plastic bottles) to implementing wholly new business models (e.g. loop), to using their voice in marketing to address important issues such as gender equality (e.g. "The best men can be", "Like A Girl"), and equality & inclusion (e.g. "The Words Matter", "Love Over Bias").

GRADUATE VACANCIES IN 2023

ENGINEERING
FINANCE
LOGISTICS
MARKETING
RESEARCH & DEVELOPMENT
SALES
TECHNOLOGY

NUMBER OF VACANCIES
50 graduate jobs

LOCATIONS OF VACANCIES

Vacancies also available in Europe.

STARTING SALARY FOR 2023
£Competitive

WORK EXPERIENCE

DEGREE PLACEMENTS | SUMMER INTERNSHIPS

UNIVERSITY PROMOTIONS DURING 2022-2023
ABERDEEN, ASTON, BATH, BIRMINGHAM, BRISTOL, BRUNEL, CAMBRIDGE, CARDIFF, DURHAM, EDINBURGH, EXETER, GLASGOW, IMPERIAL COLLEGE LONDON, KING'S COLLEGE LONDON, KENT, LANCASTER, LEEDS, LEICESTER, LIVERPOOL, LSE, LOUGHBOROUGH, MANCHESTER, NEWCASTLE, NORTHUMBRIA, NOTTINGHAM, NOTTINGHAM TRENT, OXFORD, OXFORD BROOKES, QMUL, SHEFFIELD, SOUTHAMPTON, ST ANDREWS, STRATHCLYDE, SUSSEX, UEA, UCL, WARWICK, YORK

MINIMUM ENTRY REQUIREMENTS
Varies by function
Relevant degree required for some roles.

APPLICATION DEADLINE
Varies by function

FURTHER INFORMATION
www.Top100GraduateEmployers.com
Register now for the latest news, local promotions, work experience and graduate vacancies at P&G.

Do something that matters from Day 1

To learn more about a career at P&G visit **pgcareers.com**

CLIENTS COME TO US BECAUSE WE'RE TACKLING THE MOST CHALLENGING PROBLEMS.

WE ONLY DO THE HARD STUFF AND IT'S INCREDIBLY REWARDING.

PA Consulting is a home for innovators and change-makers – blending art and science to solve the world's most complex challenges. The work PA does brings multi-disciplinary teams together who pioneer change and see the possible in the impossible.

PA Consulting is a business looking for graduates who want to make an impact. There are many compelling opportunities for early talent over a variety of sectors. At PA, early talent are encouraged to be curious, and are asked to contribute their ideas. In return, PA enables opportunities to learn from brilliant people, a supportive culture which allows people to bring their whole selves to work, and stimulating projects that improve people's lives.

PA's people are the inspiration for its purpose: bringing ingenuity to life. They focus on the future, pioneering change and always innovating. Breaking new ground on varied and purposeful projects is a cornerstone of PA's success. Partnering with clients, they deliver work that creates a fairer society and positively impacts the environment – such as collaborating with global law enforcement to prevent online abuse, designing, manufacturing and delivering thousands of ventilators to those who needed them during the fight against COVID-19, and prototyping an Electric Vehicle charge point, featured at COP26.

There are several structured programmes which graduates can consider. In Consulting, the Business Transformation and Strategy & Analytics rotational schemes allow early talent to experience a variety of teams over an 18-month period before deciding where to focus their career. There are also specialised opportunities for technical experts to join the Digital, Design, Science & Engineering sectors.

To join PA is to build a positive human future.

GRADUATE VACANCIES IN 2023
CONSULTING
ENGINEERING
RESEARCH & DEVELOPMENT
TECHNOLOGY

NUMBER OF VACANCIES
150+ graduate jobs

LOCATIONS OF VACANCIES

STARTING SALARY FOR 2023
£Competitive

WORK EXPERIENCE
DEGREE PLACEMENTS   SUMMER INTERNSHIPS

UNIVERSITY PROMOTIONS DURING 2022-2023
Please check with your university careers service for full details of PA Consulting's local promotions and events.

MINIMUM ENTRY REQUIREMENTS
Varies by function
Relevant degree required for some roles.

APPLICATION DEADLINE
Varies by function

FURTHER INFORMATION
www.Top100GraduateEmployers.com
Register now for the latest news, local promotions, work experience and graduate vacancies at PA Consulting.

PA REALLY ENCOURAGES [U]S TO TAKE HOLD OF OUR CAREER AND SEEK VARIETY.

YOU GET HANDS-ON CLIENT INTERACTION AND EXPOSURE FROM DAY ONE.

Bringing Ingenuity to Life

[p]aconsulting.com/careers

Penguin Random House UK connects the world with the stories, ideas, and writing that matter. As the biggest publisher in the UK, the diversity of its publishing includes brands such as Jamie Oliver, James Patterson, and Peppa Pig through to literary prize winners such as Zadie Smith and Richard Flanagan.

Career opportunities range from the creative teams in Editorial, Marketing, Publicity, and Design through to teams in Digital, Finance, Technology, Sales, and Publishing Operations, to name but a few.

The Scheme is Penguin Random House's flagship entry-level programme which offers 6-month traineeships to applicants who are Black, Asian, or from Minority Ethnic backgrounds and/or low socioeconomic backgrounds.

They also run 8-week Summer Internships that are open to all and offer the chance to work in teams from all departments: editorial, marketing, sales, and technology. For any vacancies or entry level programmes, there is no degree or educational requirement.

Penguin Random House has nine publishing houses – each distinct, with their own imprints, markets, and identity – including a fast-growing Audio publishing division.

They work with a wide range of talent: from storytellers, animators, and developers to entrepreneurs, toy manufacturers, producers, and – of course – writers. Just like broadcasters, they find increasingly different ways to bring stories and ideas to life.

Penguin Random House UK has two publishing sites in London – Vauxhall Bridge Road and Embassy Gardens; distribution centres in Frating, Grantham, and Rugby; and a number of regional offices. They employ over 2,000 people in the UK.

GRADUATE VACANCIES IN 2023

MARKETING

MEDIA

SALES

NUMBER OF VACANCIES
200+ entry-level roles

LOCATIONS OF VACANCIES

STARTING SALARY FOR 2023
£24,000

WORK EXPERIENCE
SUMMER
INTERNSHIPS

**UNIVERSITY PROMOTIONS
DURING 2022-2023**
*Please check with your university careers
service for full details of Penguin Random
House's local promotions and events.*

APPLICATION DEADLINE
Year-round recruitment

FURTHER INFORMATION
www.Top100GraduateEmployers.com
*Register now for the latest news, local
promotions, work experience and
graduate vacancies at Penguin.*

Your Story Starts Here

Finding a great story - editor, publisher, sales director, finance team. Making it look good - designer, copy writer, art director, illustrator. Making the finished book - production controller, product manager, quality controller. Getting it out there - marketing assistant, publicity manager, sales executive, social media manager.

Come and be part of the first of a new kind of publisher that captures the attention of the world through the stories, ideas and writing that matter.

Penguin
Random House
UK

PepsiCo is on a mission to create more smiles with every sip and bite with some of the world's favourite brands, such as Walkers, Pepsi Max, Quaker, Doritos and Sensations – to name just a few! In fact, their products are enjoyed by consumers more than one billion times a day!

PepsiCo UK has over 4,500 employees which are spread across 10 UK sites. Their vision is to be the global leader in convenient foods and beverages by winning with PepsiCo Positive. Behind this vision lies a passion for sustainability and a commitment to doing business in the right way.

PepsiCo believe that delivering for their consumers and customers, protecting the environment, sourcing with integrity, and investing in their employees is not just the right thing to do, but that these actions also position PepsiCo for long-term, sustainable growth. They're strong individualists who thrive on collaboration. To PepsiCo, it's all about respect for one another's unique traits, backgrounds, perspectives and experiences. Their teams reflect the diversity of their consumers and communities, breaking down barriers, shattering glass ceilings and winning awards.

At PepsiCo, graduates get the best of both worlds: an entrepreneur's mindset plus reach and resources. Their collaborative culture and worldwide presence generate a stream of new opportunities to define the future and propel their team's life's work.

PepsiCo are looking for Future Leaders to join their 3-year Dare to Do More graduate programme in Sales, Marketing, Digital or Insights, who want the opportunity to fast-track their career within a leading global brand. Bring a unique perspective. Bring curiosity. Bring ingenuity, and drive. PepsiCo give graduates a platform to be daring on a global scale.

GRADUATE VACANCIES IN 2023

MARKETING

SALES

NUMBER OF VACANCIES
15-20 graduate jobs

LOCATIONS OF VACANCIES

STARTING SALARY FOR 2023
£30,000
Plus a relocation allowance.

WORK EXPERIENCE

DEGREE PLACEMENTS | SUMMER INTERNSHIPS

UNIVERSITY PROMOTIONS DURING 2022-2023
ASTON, BATH, BIRMINGHAM, BRISTOL, CARDIFF, CITY, EDINBURGH, EXETER, GLASGOW, LANCASTER, LEEDS, LEICESTER, LIVERPOOL, LOUGHBOROUGH, MANCHESTER, NOTTINGHAM, NOTTINGHAM TRENT, QUEEN MARY LONDON, READING, SHEFFIELD, SOUTHAMPTON
Please check with your university careers service for full details of PepsiCo's local promotions and events.

MINIMUM ENTRY REQUIREMENTS
Any degree accepted

APPLICATION DEADLINE
26th October 2022

FURTHER INFORMATION
www.Top100GraduateEmployers.com
Register now for the latest news, local promotions, work experience and graduate vacancies at PepsiCo.

DO YOU DARE TO BE...

CURIOUS?

CREATIVE?

BOLD?

PEPSICO

DARE TO DO MORE
GLOBAL STUDENT CHALLENGE

daretodomoreeurope.pepsico.com/en

POLICE:NOW
INFLUENCE FOR GENERATIONS

PoliceNow **f**   graduates@policenow.org.uk ✉

@Police_Now **𝕏**   linkedin.com/school/police-now **in**

@PoliceNowGraduates **⊙**   youtube.com/PoliceNowChangeTheStory **▶**

DIV
ERS
ITY

Police Now is an independent social enterprise that seeks to ignite change through its mission; to transform communities, reduce crime and increase the public's confidence in the police service by recruiting, developing and inspiring outstanding diverse individuals to be leaders in society and on the policing frontline.

Police Now is dedicated to attracting and developing the most diverse group of officers into policing, especially those who have not previously considered policing as a career. Nationally, 25% of participants who began the National Graduate Leadership Programme in 2021 identify as from a Black, Asian or minority ethnic background and 52% as women. Of those who began the National Detective Programme in 2021, 24% identify as from a Black, Asian or minority ethnic background and 66% as women.

Police Now's national graduate programmes offer the ability to lay the foundations for a successful long-term career in policing, by providing graduates with the ability to strive for change and to make an immediate and real impact in their community. During the two years, graduates will expand their knowledge of the policing sector, starting with an intensive training academy led by policing professionals with years of experience, whilst working towards their Graduate Diploma in Professional Policing Practice.

After successfully completing the two-year programme, it does not stop there. Police Now's graduate programmes offer more than a job, but a career for life, with ongoing development beyond the programme and an ongoing connection with Police Now during their time in the service and if graduates choose to move into other sectors.

Develop skills for life, whilst making a positive impact on society and improving local communities.

GRADUATE VACANCIES IN 2023
POLICING

NUMBER OF VACANCIES
400+ graduate jobs

LOCATIONS OF VACANCIES

STARTING SALARY FOR 2023
£24,780-£31,686

UNIVERSITY PROMOTIONS DURING 2022-2023
Please check with your university careers service for full details of Police Now's local promotions and events.

MINIMUM ENTRY REQUIREMENTS
2.1 Degree

APPLICATION DEADLINE
Varies by function
Please see website for full details.

FURTHER INFORMATION
www.Top100GraduateEmployers.com
Register now for the latest news, local promotions, work experience and graduate vacancies at **Police Now**.

Want more?

pwc

pwc.co.uk/careers

PwCcareersUK   UK_HC-Services-Student-Recruitment@pwc.com

@PwC_UK_careers   linkedin.com/company/pwc-uk **in**

@PwC_UK_careers ⃝   youtube.com/careersPwC ▶

PwC's purpose is to build trust in society and solve important problems. Helping clients and communities address the biggest challenges they face has never been more important. Join Actuarial, Audit, Business Solutions, Consulting, Deals, Legal, Risk, Tax or Technology.

PwCs global strategy, called The New Equation, brings its purpose to life by bringing its people together to strive for imaginative ways of solving their clients' most important challenges. They're investing in the areas that matter most. Building out their capabilities in ESG and Net Zero, and combining the diverse experiences and skills of their people with innovative technology to build trust and deliver sustained outcomes.

Employing 24,000 people across the UK, attracting, retaining and investing in the best people is critical. In some areas, this could mean working towards a professional qualification. In return, they ask that joiners are eager to learn, with business awareness, intellectual and cultural curiosity and the ability to build strong relationships. They encourage their people to work together, share knowledge and insights that foster innovation, drive impact and deliver quality to their clients.

Graduates and undergraduates can expect to be part of a stimulating environment working on challenging projects in a culture that embraces difference and empowers them to think differently. Their uniqueness and innovation is valued at PwC which is why they have The Deal for all employees that ensures the experience of working there is right for everyone. Their hard work and accomplishments will be recognised and rewarded with a competitive salary and tailored, flexible benefits. Join a diverse community of solvers. Be a part of The New Equation.

GRADUATE VACANCIES IN 2023

ACCOUNTANCY
CONSULTING
FINANCE
LAW
TECHNOLOGY

NUMBER OF VACANCIES
1,800+ graduate jobs

LOCATIONS OF VACANCIES

STARTING SALARY FOR 2023
£Competitive

WORK EXPERIENCE

| INSIGHT COURSES | DEGREE PLACEMENTS | SUMMER INTERNSHIPS |

UNIVERSITY PROMOTIONS DURING 2022-2023
ABERDEEN, ABERYSTWYTH, ASTON, BANGOR, BATH, BELFAST, BIRMINGHAM, BRADFORD, BRISTOL, BRUNEL, CAMBRIDGE, CARDIFF, CITY, DUNDEE, DURHAM, EDINBURGH, ESSEX, EXETER, GLASGOW, HERIOT-WATT, HULL, IMPERIAL COLLEGE LONDON, KEELE, KING'S COLLEGE LONDON, KENT, LANCASTER, LEEDS, LEICESTER, LIVERPOOL, LONDON SCHOOL OF ECONOMICS, LOUGHBOROUGH, MANCHESTER, NEWCASTLE, NORTHUMBRIA, NOTTINGHAM, NOTTINGHAM TRENT, OXFORD, OXFORD BROOKES, PLYMOUTH, QUEEN MARY LONDON, READING, ROYAL HOLLOWAY, SCHOOL OF AFRICAN STUDIES, SHEFFIELD, SOUTHAMPTON, ST ANDREWS, STIRLING, STRATHCLYDE, SURREY, SUSSEX, SWANSEA, UEA, ULSTER, UNIVERSITY COLLEGE LONDON, WARWICK, YORK

MINIMUM ENTRY REQUIREMENTS
Any degree accepted

APPLICATION DEADLINE
Varies by function

FURTHER INFORMATION
www.Top100GraduateEmployers.com
Register now for the latest news, local promotions, work experience and graduate vacancies at PwC.

Kun's story

2021

Certified in Alteryx
Advanced level

2021

Became solution lead for a
group scoping tool

2021

Transferred to digital audit
advanced analytics

2017

Joined PwC's Graduate
Audit programme

2016

Joined PwC's Women in
Business programme

Join our community of solvers

Kun first joined PwC on our Women in Business programme and
rejoined as an audit associate after graduation. After qualifying
as a chartered accountant, she wanted to pursue her passion for
technology and now uses her ACA qualification to provide vital
insight in creating bespoke solutions for our clients.

Be a part of The New Equation

To find out more, visit: **pwc.co.uk/careers**

ReedSmith

graduate.recruitment@reedsmith.com

@ReedSmithLLP 🐦 linkedin.com/company/reed-smith-llp 💼

@ReedSmithGrads 📷 youtube.com/ReedSmithLLP ▶

Reed Smith is a dynamic, international law firm dedicated to helping clients move their businesses forward. With an inclusive and innovative mindset, they deliver smarter, more creative legal services that drive better outcomes for their clients, communities and team.

Reed Smith operates as one global partnership and has more than 3,000 employees (including more than 1,700 lawyers) across 30 offices in the United States, Europe, the Middle East and Asia. Their deep industry knowledge spans energy and natural resources, financial services, life sciences and healthcare, entertainment and media and transportation. This, paired with their long-standing relationships and collaborative structure, makes them the go-to partner for complex disputes, transactions and regulatory matters.

Ambitious and entrepreneurial graduates are rewarded at Reed Smith with a training programme that is supportive, challenging and exciting, offering unparalleled pro bono, client and international secondments. They are also amongst the first firms to offer a unique approach to the Solicitor's Qualifying Examination with their brand new Professional SQE programme. Future trainees will gain experience in the firm's numerous business services teams whilst also studying for their exams, providing them with invaluable insight into the work they do across the firm.

Their unique culture, which allows trainees to turn passions into careers, is one of the reasons their lawyers remain with the firm for such a long time, moving seats, job roles and even countries as their careers with the firm develop. Reed Smith are recruiting creative and forward-thinking graduates who like to take initiative and drive progress. Graduates can apply now to be the next generation of law at Reed Smith.

GRADUATE VACANCIES IN 2023
`LAW`

NUMBER OF VACANCIES
25 graduate jobs
For training contracts starting in 2025.

LOCATIONS OF VACANCIES

STARTING SALARY FOR 2023
£50,000
Sponsorship of Law Conversion Course and Solicitors Qualifying Exam Maintenance grant of £9,000 and £10,000 respectively.

WORK EXPERIENCE
`INSIGHT COURSES`

UNIVERSITY PROMOTIONS DURING 2022-2023
ASTON, BATH, BIRMINGHAM, BRISTOL, CITY, DURHAM, ESSEX, EXETER, HULL, IMPERIAL COLLEGE LONDON, KING'S COLLEGE LONDON, KENT, LEEDS, LEICESTER, LIVERPOOL, LONDON SCHOOL OF ECONOMICS, MANCHESTER, NEWCASTLE, NOTTINGHAM, QUEEN MARY LONDON, READING, ROYAL HOLLOWAY, SHEFFIELD, SOUTHAMPTON, ST ANDREWS, SURREY, SUSSEX, UEA, UNIVERSITY COLLEGE LONDON, WARWICK, YORK
Please check with your university careers service for full details of Reed Smith's local promotions and events.

MINIMUM ENTRY REQUIREMENTS
2.1 Degree

APPLICATION DEADLINE
Early October - Middle December

FURTHER INFORMATION
www.Top100GraduateEmployers.com
Register now for the latest news, local promotions, work experience and graduate vacancies at Reed Smith.

Rolls-Royce pioneers cutting-edge technologies to deliver the cleanest, safest and most competitive solutions to the planet's vital power needs. From developing products that are powering all-electric aircrafts to discovering solutions for space exploration. A career at Rolls-Royce means shaping the future.

Pioneers do things differently. So, a career at Rolls-Royce means challenging the status quo and continually re-shaping what's possible. And because different ways of thinking make for better, bolder ideas, candidates who join the business at this exciting point in its history, will be joining a diversely talented, global workforce dedicated to that mission.

Focused on meeting the planet's vital energy needs as well as its own net zero carbon ambitions, Rolls-Royce believes now is the time to act as one community and one business. That means recognising the unique talents of each individual across the organisation – celebrating and rewarding them, supporting and developing them, empowering them in every way to thrive and succeed.

For candidates from STEM and Business with STEM disciplines, Rolls-Royce offers a wide range of graduate and internship opportunities, including a Grad Directs programme that enables them to start immediately in a designated role. Whether it's focused on developing leadership capabilities, or striving for the next big technological breakthrough, each opportunity offers the chance to build an impactful and rewarding career.

While individuality is valued at Rolls-Royce, there are certain qualities the company looks for in everyone who works there. Agility, creativity and innovation are key. As are a boldness of spirit and a genuine passion for the work they do. But perhaps most important are an open-mind, a collaborative approach and the ability to bring a fresh perspective to each new challenge.

GRADUATE VACANCIES IN 2023
ENGINEERING
GENERAL MANAGEMENT
TECHNOLOGY

NUMBER OF VACANCIES
No fixed quota

LOCATIONS OF VACANCIES

STARTING SALARY FOR 2023
£28,500

UNIVERSITY PROMOTIONS DURING 2022-2023
Please check with your university careers service for full details of Rolls-Royce's local promotions and events.

MINIMUM ENTRY REQUIREMENTS
Varies by function
Relevant degree required for some roles.

APPLICATION DEADLINE
Year-round recruitment
Early application is advised

FURTHER INFORMATION
www.Top100GraduateEmployers.com
*Register now for the latest news, local promotions, work experience and graduate vacancies at **Rolls-Royce**.*

Bring everything you are
& build a bright future

At Rolls-Royce, we pioneer the power that matters. As one of the few global companies best positioned to shape the future of power and reduce its impact on the world, we're focused on meeting the planet's vital energy needs while achieving our net zero carbon ambitions.

To do this, we need people with diverse talents and ways of looking at the world. Which is why we offer a variety of early careers opportunities, from summer internships and graduate programmes – including options that enable you to move around and try different things or jump straight in to your first role – to our diversity-focused i-Accelerator programme for data, tech and AI.

Visit careers.rolls-royce.com

PIONEERS OF POWER

Throughout the course of history, a life at sea has always attracted those with a taste for travel and adventure; but there are plenty of other reasons for graduates and final-year students to consider a challenging and wide-ranging career with the Royal Navy.

The Royal Navy is, first and foremost, a fighting force. Serving alongside Britain's allies in conflicts around the world, it also vitally protects UK ports, fishing grounds, and merchant ships, helping to combat international smuggling, terrorism, and piracy. Increasingly, its 30,000 personnel are involved in humanitarian and relief missions; situations where their skills, discipline, and resourcefulness make a real difference to people's lives.

Graduates are able to join the Royal Navy as Officers – the senior leadership and management team in the various branches, which range from engineering, air, and warfare to medical, the Fleet Air Arm, and logistics. Starting salaries of at least £27,000 – rising to approximately £33,000 in the second year – compare well with those in industry.

Those wanting to join the Royal Navy as an Engineer – with Marine, Weapon, or Air Engineer Officer, above or below the water – could work on anything from sensitive electronics to massive gas-turbine engines and nuclear weapons. What's more, the Royal Navy can offer a secure, flexible career and the potential to extend to age 50.

The Royal Navy offers opportunities for early responsibility, career development, sport, recreation, and travel which exceed any in civilian life. With its global reach and responsibilities, the Royal Navy still offers plenty of adventure and the chance to see the world, while pursuing one of the most challenging, varied, and fulfilling careers available.

GRADUATE VACANCIES IN 2023
ENGINEERING
FINANCE
GENERAL MANAGEMENT
HUMAN RESOURCES
LAW
LOGISTICS
MEDIA
RESEARCH & DEVELOPMENT
TECHNOLOGY

NUMBER OF VACANCIES
No fixed quota

LOCATIONS OF VACANCIES

Vacancies also available elsewhere in the world.

STARTING SALARY FOR 2023
£27,000
Some roles offering a £27,000 joining bonus.

WORK EXPERIENCE
INSIGHT COURSES DEGREE PLACEMENTS SUMMER INTERNSHIPS

UNIVERSITY PROMOTIONS DURING 2022 -2023
Please check with your university careers service for full details of the Royal Navy's local promotions and events.

MINIMUM ENTRY REQUIREMENTS
Relevant degree required for some roles.

APPLICATION DEADLINE
Year-round recruitment

FURTHER INFORMATION
www.Top100GraduateEmployers.com
Register now for the latest news, local promotions, work experience and graduate vacancies at the Royal Navy.

A CAREER THAT MAKES
A WORLD OF DIFFERENCE

A career in the Royal Navy is like no other. A job where no two days are the same, where you can challenge yourself and solve problems on the go. Plus, you get to travel the world, all while helping those that are in need.

For more information call 0345 607 5555
Visit royalnavy.mod.uk/careers

Santander

santander.com/en/careers

emergingtalent@santander.co.uk

Aside from Santander being a bank, they're also part of one of the world's leading financial groups with 140 million customers worldwide. They've invested over 98 million euros into training and developing their people. Not only that, but they love nothing more than setting graduate potential free.

As a digital bank leading with technology, Santander has its sights on being the best open financial services platform, launching Digital Consumer Bank, intending to be the largest of its kind in the world. In response to today's demand, their engineers create cutting-edge digital services and applications for their customers across the retail and commercial banks, brought to life through access to the newest cloud-based innovative technologies.

They deliver outstanding services from exceptional people, inspired and motivated by collaboration, respect and market-leading benefits and incentives packages. It's all made possible by a culture that supports and nurtures people as they deliver their personal best every day.

Santander's Emerging Talent programmes are about bringing together talented people from a diverse range of backgrounds to make it happen. And as they embrace change, drive innovation and develop as a business, there'll be opportunities for talent to grow too.

Their graduate programme provides a solid grounding to kick-start a career. So, for those committed to making things simple, personal, and fair for customers and colleagues, bringing passion to the role, there's no better place to unleash ambition. Through these programmes graduates will have all of the support they need in order to succeed, with a dedicated graduate manager as well as continuous development – there's plenty of benefits and no shortage of opportunities to grow with Santander.

GRADUATE VACANCIES IN 2023

FINANCE
INVESTMENT BANKING
RETAIL
TECHNOLOGY

NUMBER OF VACANCIES
80 graduate jobs

LOCATIONS OF VACANCIES

STARTING SALARY FOR 2023
£30,000-£44,000

WORK EXPERIENCE
SUMMER
INTERNSHIPS

UNIVERSITY PROMOTIONS DURING 2022-2023
Please check with your university careers service for full details of Santander's local promotions and events.

MINIMUM ENTRY REQUIREMENTS
Varies by function
Relevant degree required for some roles.

APPLICATION DEADLINE
Varies by function

FURTHER INFORMATION
www.Top100GraduateEmployers.com
*Register now for the latest news, local promotions, work experience and graduate vacancies at **Santander**.*

savills.co.uk/graduates

@SavillsInstaGrad gradrecruitment@savills.com

Savills is a world leading property agent, employing over 39,000 people across 600 offices. Their expertise spans the globe and they offer wide-ranging specialist knowledge. Savills take pride in providing best-in-class advice as they help individuals, businesses and institutions make better property decisions.

Savills passionately believe that their graduates are future leaders, and as such make a huge investment in them. At Savills, their best asset is their people and supporting people to enable them to be the best version of themselves is at the heart of the business. Savills graduates are given responsibility from day one, in teams who highly value their contribution, allowing them to be involved in some of the world's most high-profile property deals and developments. Graduates are surrounded by expert professionals and experienced team members from whom they learn and seek advice. Individual achievement is rewarded, and Savills look for bold graduates with entrepreneurial flair.

Savills are proud to have won The Times Graduate Recruitment Award: Employer of Choice for Property for the sixteenth year running. A great work-life balance, structured training and a dynamic working environment are amongst the factors which see Savills wining The Times Graduate Employer of choice for Property year-on-year.

Savills' Graduate Programme offers the chance to gain internationally recognised professional qualifications. The company offers roles within Surveying, Planning, Sustainability, Food & Farming and Forestry, with half of these vacancies in regional locations. The company has offices in exciting locations around the UK, where Fee Earners work with varied and prestigious clients. The diversity of Savills services means there is the flexibility to carve out a fulfilling, self-tailored career path in any location.

GRADUATE VACANCIES IN 2023
PROPERTY

NUMBER OF VACANCIES
150+ graduate jobs

LOCATIONS OF VACANCIES

STARTING SALARY FOR 2023
£25,000-£28,000
Plus a discretionary annual bonus.

WORK EXPERIENCE
INSIGHT COURSES | DEGREE PLACEMENTS | SUMMER INTERNSHIPS

UNIVERSITY PROMOTIONS DURING 2022-2023
ABERDEEN, BATH, BIRMINGHAM, BRISTOL, CAMBRIDGE, CARDIFF, CITY, DURHAM, EDINBURGH, EXETER, GLASGOW, HERIOT-WATT, IMPERIAL COLLEGE LONDON, KING'S COLLEGE LONDON, LEEDS, LONDON SCHOOL OF ECONOMICS, LOUGHBOROUGH, MANCHESTER, NEWCASTLE, NORTHUMBRIA, NOTTINGHAM, NOTTINGHAM TRENT, OXFORD, OXFORD BROOKES, READING, SHEFFIELD, SOUTHAMPTON, SUSSEX, UNIVERSITY COLLEGE LONDON, YORK.
Please check with your university careers service for full details of Savills local promotions and events.

MINIMUM ENTRY REQUIREMENTS
Varies by function
Relevant degree required for some roles.

APPLICATION DEADLINE
Mid-November

FURTHER INFORMATION
www.Top100GraduateEmployers.com
Register now for the latest news, local promotions, work experience and graduate vacancies at Savills.

SHAPE YOUR FUTURE

"I was involved in high profile planning projects of between 2000 and 4000 homes within the first 6 months of joining Savills"

"I assisted with successfully pitching for the disposal of a portfolio of logistics assets across Northern Europe worth approximately €400 million"

"I have helped progress over 300 Megawatts of energy for the UK power grid through renewable developments - enough to power nearly 200,000 homes"

18
possible career paths

2-3
year training programme with permanent employment contract

16
Years as The Times Graduate Employer of Choice for Property

40%
of our main board joined as graduate trainees

39,000+
global employees

600+
offices in over 70 countries

A career in real estate offers an exciting and dynamic career path with the opportunity to specialise in several different areas that help shape the future of our built environment.

Become **the future of Savills**

@ @savillsinstagrad   #careersinproperty

Shell is an international energy company that aims to meet the world's growing need for more and cleaner energy solutions in ways that are economically, environmentally and socially responsible. It is one of the world's largest independent energy companies, operating in more than 70 countries.

Shell has a global target to become a net zero emissions energy business by 2050. This means that Shell aims to be net zero on all emissions generated by its operations and the energy needed to power them. The company is working with customers, business, and governments to address emissions across different sectors.

In March 2022, Shell UK announced an ambition to invest between £20 to £25 billion in the UK energy system over the next decade, more than 75% of which is intended for low and zero-carbon products and services including offshore wind, hydrogen and electric mobility. These investments, which are subject to board approval, aim to propel the UK closer to net zero whilst intending to stimulate economic growth and jobs.

Shell interns and graduates can help drive innovation and develop tomorrow's energy solutions today. No matter their discipline, their work will be contributing to the global transition to more and cleaner energy, where their unique ideas and perspective will be encouraged. They will have the opportunity to propel their careers to new heights and be part of an organisation that changes the global energy system and shapes the future.

Shell is looking for graduates who share their purpose to power progress. Their inclusive and collaborative culture will equip graduates with the support they need to forge their own path, and work on meaningful projects right from the start.

GRADUATE VACANCIES IN 2023
ENGINEERING
FINANCE
GENERAL MANAGEMENT
HUMAN RESOURCES
RESEARCH & DEVELOPMENT
TECHNOLOGY

NUMBER OF VACANCIES
70+ graduate jobs

LOCATIONS OF VACANCIES

STARTING SALARY FOR 2023
£Competitive

WORK EXPERIENCE
SUMMER INTERNSHIPS

UNIVERSITY PROMOTIONS DURING 2022-2023
ABERDEEN, CAMBRIDGE, HERIOT-WATT, IMPERIAL COLLEGE LONDON, LEEDS, LONDON SCHOOL OF ECONOMICS, OXFORD, QUEEN MARY LONDON, STRATHCLYDE, UNIVERSITY COLLEGE LONDON, WARWICK
Please check with your university careers service for full details of Shell's local promotions and events.

MINIMUM ENTRY REQUIREMENTS
Varies by function
Relevant degree required for some roles.

APPLICATION DEADLINE
December 2022

FURTHER INFORMATION
www.Top100GraduateEmployers.com
Register now for the latest news, local promotions, work experience and graduate vacancies at Shell.

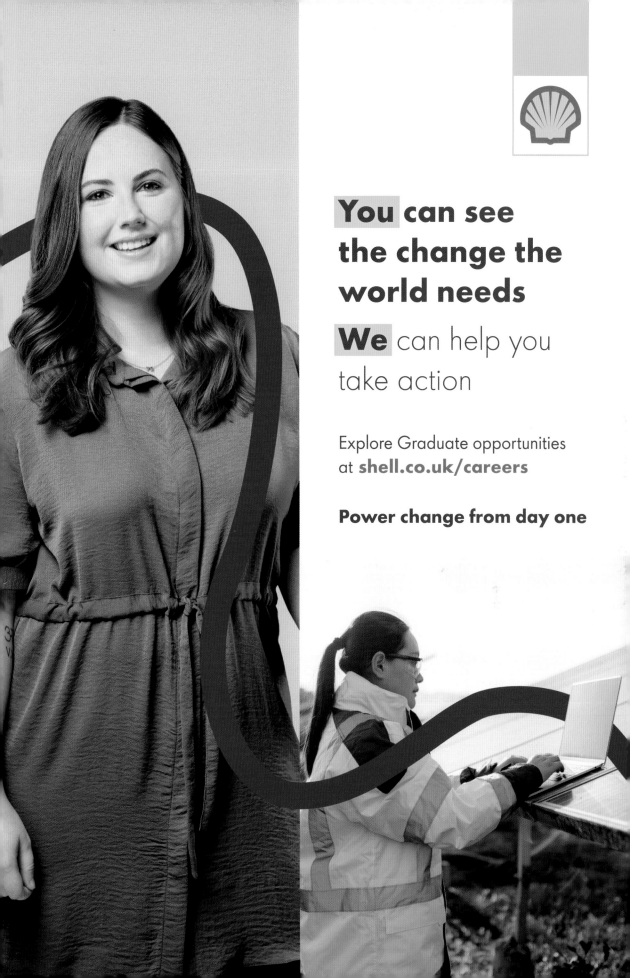

EarlyCareersSky **f**   earlycareers@sky.uk ✉

@EarlyCareersSky 🐦 linkedin.com/company/sky **in**

@_ LifeAtSky 📷 youtube.com/lifeatsky ▶

Sky is Europe's leading media and entertainment company and is proud to be part of Comcast Corporation, connecting people to the moments that matter. Across six countries, Sky connects 23 million customers to the best entertainment, sports, news, arts and their own award-winning original content.

Passionate about building tech that improves how the world watches sport? Keen to pick up heaps of new skills trying out lots of different functions? Want to work in finance and support the future of the world's favourite shows? At Sky graduates can.

The range of graduate programmes at Sky gives new joiners the chance to do all this and more. Their graduates can make a real impact – owning projects that push not only their development, but the future of Sky too. Sky has a range of graduate programmes from technology, cyber security to finance or business strategy. Sky also offers internships and all year round insight events designed to give graduates a sneak peek at life at Sky.

So, whatever background, skills or passions, graduates can choose a career path that suits them. Graduates are surrounded by some of the best people in the industry. They will benefit from on-the-job learning, and receive the support they need to be brilliant at what they do.

Sky is a place where people from all walks of life get the freedom and support to do their best work. The business takes pride in their approach to diversity and inclusion: they've been recognised by The Times and Stonewall for their commitment to diversity, and they've set ambitious 2025 targets to continue to increase diversity and representation. They're also committed to investing £30 million across their markets over the next three years to improve their approach to diversity and inclusion, and to tackle racial injustice.

GRADUATE VACANCIES IN 2023

ACCOUNTANCY

ENGINEERING

FINANCE

GENERAL MANAGEMENT

MARKETING

MEDIA

SALES

TECHNOLOGY

NUMBER OF VACANCIES
170+ graduate jobs

LOCATIONS OF VACANCIES

STARTING SALARY FOR 2023
£28,000-£38,000

WORK EXPERIENCE
INSIGHT COURSES   SUMMER INTERNSHIPS

UNIVERSITY PROMOTIONS DURING 2022-2023
ABERDEEN, ASTON, BATH, BELFAST, BIRMINGHAM, BRISTOL, BRUNEL, CARDIFF, CITY, DUNDEE, EDINBURGH, ESSEX, EXETER, HULL, IMPERIAL COLLEGE LONDON, KING'S COLLEGE LONDON, KENT, LEEDS, LEICESTER, LIVERPOOL, MANCHESTER, NEWCASTLE, NOTTINGHAM, NOTTINGHAM TRENT, QUEEN MARY LONDON, READING, SHEFFIELD, SOUTHAMPTON, STRATHCLYDE, SURREY, SUSSEX, UNIVERSITY COLLEGE LONDON, WARWICK, YORK

MINIMUM ENTRY REQUIREMENTS
Any degree accepted

APPLICATION DEADLINE
Varies by function

FURTHER INFORMATION
www.Top100GraduateEmployers.com
Register now for the latest news, local promotions, work experience and graduate vacancies at Sky.

You can be who
You want to be

We celebrate diversity. Because different people with different perspectives make Sky a better business. Our customers are incredibly diverse, so we should be too. That's why we're working hard to build an inclusive culture, where you can be yourself. Whoever you are. Wherever you're from.

Launch an exciting career with Sky, Europe's largest media company – our graduate programmes cover a wide range of exciting areas including Business Strategy, Finance, Change Delivery, Technology, Software Engineering and much more.

Find out about all our Early Careers opportunities at:
skyearlycareers.com

A job you love to talk about

sky

SLAUGHTER AND MAY/

slaughterandmay.com

trainee.recruit@slaughterandmay.com

@SlaughterandMayCareers

Slaughter and May is one of the most prestigious law firms in the world. The strength of their global practice is reflected both in the multi-jurisdictional nature of their work and their international client base. The firm is a trusted adviser to some of the largest global companies in the world.

There are distinct differences that set Slaughter and May apart from other global law firms. These differences are in relation to their international approach, multi-specialist training, and lack of billable targets.

Slaughter and May work with the very best law firms across the globe to support their clients, handpicked to meet the needs of each matter, to deliver integrated legal advice. Fundamental to their business model is the ability to work in partnership with other law firms – this is how they have built their successful global practice.

Slaughter and May lawyers are all trained to be multi-specialists across a broad range of legal matters. This is hard work, but their lawyers say it makes for a far more fulfilling career. It provides challenge and interest and also allows their lawyers to develop deeper relationships with clients, because they get to know their businesses better.

Their lawyers are not set billing targets. In this way, their lawyers are free to work collaboratively, sharing expertise and knowledge so that they can concentrate on what matters most – the quality of the work and client service.

Slaughter and May takes great store in drawing strength from diversity and believes that an inclusive workplace drives collaboration and enhances business performance. They are looking to employ the brightest minds regardless of what or where they studied. They offer open days, workshops, and work experience schemes to enable applicants to gain an insight into life as a commercial lawyer.

GRADUATE VACANCIES IN 2023

LAW

NUMBER OF VACANCIES
85 graduate jobs
For training contracts starting in 2025.

LOCATIONS OF VACANCIES

STARTING SALARY FOR 2023
£50,000

WORK EXPERIENCE
INSIGHT COURSES   SUMMER INTERNSHIPS

UNIVERSITY PROMOTIONS DURING 2022-2023
Please check with your university careers service for full details of Slaughter and May's local promotions and events.

MINIMUM ENTRY REQUIREMENTS
2.1 Degree

APPLICATION DEADLINE
Please see website for full details.

FURTHER INFORMATION
www.Top100GraduateEmployers.com
Register now for the latest news, local promotions, work experience and graduate vacancies at Slaughter and May.

LifeatSpecsavers **f** uk.resourcing@specsavers.com ✉

@SpecsaversLife **y** linkedin.com/company/specsavers **in**

@LifeatSpecsavers **O** youtube.com/LifeatSpecsavers **▶**

GRADUATE VACANCIES IN 2023
ACCOUNTANCY
FINANCE
GENERAL MANAGEMENT
HUMAN RESOURCES
MARKETING
MEDIA
RETAIL
TECHNOLOGY

NUMBER OF VACANCIES
40+ graduate jobs

LOCATIONS OF VACANCIES

Vacancies also available elsewhere in the world.

STARTING SALARY FOR 2023
£28,000
Plus competitive bonuses.

UNIVERSITY PROMOTIONS DURING 2022-2023
ASTON, BRADFORD, CARDIFF, CITY,
GLASGOW, MANCHESTER, NOTTINGHAM,
NOTTINGHAM TRENT, PLYMOUTH,
SOUTHAMPTON, UEA, ULSTER
Please check with your university careers service for full details of Specsaver's local promotions and events.

MINIMUM ENTRY REQUIREMENTS
Any degree accepted

APPLICATION DEADLINE
Varies by function

FURTHER INFORMATION
www.Top100GraduateEmployers.com
Register now for the latest news, local promotions, work experience and graduate vacancies at **Specsavers**.

Specsavers changes lives through better sight and hearing. As the largest privately-owned optical group in the world, their 40,000 colleagues make a genuine difference to communities, people and the planet. Making this difference starts with supporting graduates to change lives every single day, in a sustainable way.

Specsavers' New Talent Programme gives graduates a fast track to senior roles in clinical care, retail, business support or supply chain logistics, providing unwavering quality to 41 million customers in 11 countries, and the chance to develop leadership skills for life. Specsavers welcomes graduates from almost every degree discipline. Those who follow the 12-month support office scheme are challenged and supported through placements in marketing, technology, operations, finance, e-commerce and more, with residential experiences to expand and strengthen skillsets.

They also offer a three-year 'Beyond the Graduate' programme for optometrists to progress through Specsavers Pre-reg Academy and higher qualifications with access to funding. Audiologists are given tailored mentoring to make career dreams come true. The Specsavers family works together in stores and through the Home Visits to achieve the best possible outcome for patients. Not to mention the global opportunities on offer. Graduates could build and own a business in Canada, take a secondment in Australia or be a pioneer in a brand new Specsavers location.

At Specsavers, everybody is somebody. The diverse and inclusive culture is key to achieving long-term goals. What's more Specsavers believes in rewarding graduates for their hard work with a competitive salary and bonus, and a great mix of benefits that gives everyone the recognition they deserve. Find the perfect role and change lives through better sight and hearing, every single day.

More than just glasses

You'll know us for one thing but we're so much more.
Find out just how many opportunities we have
for an amazing and rewarding career.

TeachFirst **f**   recruitment@teachfirst.org.uk ✉

@TeachFirst **🐦**   linkedin.com/company/teach-first **in**

@TeachFirstUK **◯**   youtube.com/TeachFirstYT **▶**

Teach First

Right now, there are children in this country who won't get the education they deserve. It's not okay and it's not fair. Teach First are fighting to make the education system work for every child. Developing teachers and leaders determined to make a difference in the schools where they're needed the most.

Graduates have many career options ahead of them, but few are more meaningful than teaching. Two years of a pandemic and a critical shortage of teachers has only widened the educational inequality gap, with disadvantaged children now 18 months behind their wealthier peers when they take their GCSEs. It's clear great teachers are needed – now more than ever – to help every young person get the education they deserve.

Teach First's Training Programme is the largest teacher training and leadership programme in the UK. It offers graduates a salary while they train and opens the door to a world of career possibilities. Over two years, they'll qualify as teachers, gain a fully-funded Postgraduate Diploma in Education and Leadership (PGDE) and develop an array of transferable leadership skills.

From their first day in the classroom, trainees make an instant impact on the lives of young people, in a role where no two days are the same. With support from Teach First, trainees are seven times more likely to progress into leadership roles early in their careers. And the charity's influential network links them to a range of organisations, with many of them offering trainees extra opportunities to hone their leadership skills through coaching and summer projects.

The challenge is real, but so is the chance to create lasting change. This is the most important generation of teachers and leaders, joining Teach First to fight for a fairer future.

Visit the Teach First website to find out more and apply now.

GRADUATE VACANCIES IN 2023
TEACHING

NUMBER OF VACANCIES
1750 graduate jobs

LOCATIONS OF VACANCIES

STARTING SALARY FOR 2023
£Competitive

WORK EXPERIENCE
INSIGHT COURSES

UNIVERSITY PROMOTIONS DURING 2022-2023
ABERDEEN, ABERYSTWYTH, ASTON, BANGOR, BATH, BELFAST, BIRMINGHAM, BRADFORD, BRISTOL, CAMBRIDGE, CARDIFF, CITY, DURHAM, EDINBURGH, ESSEX, EXETER, GLASGOW, HERIOT-WATT, HULL, IMPERIAL COLLEGE LONDON, KEELE, KING'S COLLEGE LONDON, KENT, LANCASTER, LEEDS, LEICESTER, LIVERPOOL, LONDON SCHOOL OF ECONOMICS, LOUGHBOROUGH, MANCHESTER, NEWCASTLE, NORTHUMBRIA, NOTTINGHAM, NOTTINGHAM TRENT, OXFORD, OXFORD BROOKES, PLYMOUTH, QUEEN MARY LONDON, READING, ROYAL HOLLOWAY, SCHOOL OF AFRICAN STUDIES, SHEFFIELD, SOUTHAMPTON, ST ANDREWS, SURREY, SUSSEX, SWANSEA, UEA, UNIVERSITY COLLEGE LONDON, WARWICK, YORK

MINIMUM ENTRY REQUIREMENTS
2.1 Degree
However, all applications are assessed on a case-by-case basis..

APPLICATION DEADLINE
Year-round recruitment
Early application is advised.

FURTHER INFORMATION
www.Top100GraduateEmployers.com
*Register now for the latest news, local promotions, work experience and graduate vacancies at **Teach First**.*

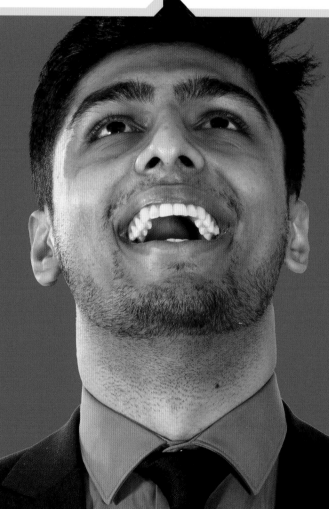

Time to

A. Take a backseat

B. Lead from the front

This is your chance to change the future. Join the most important generation of teachers and leaders to transform countless lives – starting with your own.

Apply now for our Training Programme.

CHOOSE TO LEAD

Teach First

THG

thg.com

graduates@thehutgroup.com

@THG   linkedin.com/company/thgplc

Since 2004, THG have grown from a British start-up to a globally renowned end-to-end tech platform specialising in taking brands direct to consumers worldwide, powered by their propriety technology platform, THG Ingenuity. They are headquartered in Manchester and operate across several divisions.

THG's divisions include Beauty, Nutrition, OnDemand, Luxury and THG Experience – and they employ circa 9,000 people around the world. THG's portfolio of world-leading brands is powered by its propriety end to end e-commerce platform, THG Ingenuity. THG Ingenuity also enables the digital growth of third-party clients, including Homebase, Elemis, and Nestle, who benefit from its technology, infrastructure, and brand building solutions.

With THG, graduates will go further, faster. They create unrivalled early careers opportunities by driving progression at an exceptional rate. Interns and graduates at THG will be in control of shaping their future, and that's why THG look for ambitious, driven people who display agile and innovative thinking.

Each role comes with real responsibilities, giving graduates the unique opportunity to make an impact from day one. Whether they join THG as a Graduate Software Engineer, Graduate Ecommerce Executive, or Marketing Intern, graduates will have the chance to meet new people, work with industry experts, and develop the skills required to be future leaders and technical specialists. THG are committed to supporting personal and professional development and believe that giving graduates the freedom to manage their career will help them to thrive at THG. Their 12-month graduate programme consists of in-person networking opportunities with industry experts, as well as 6-months of learning and development workshops delivered by the Early Careers team in partnership with L&D Partners across the Group.

GRADUATE VACANCIES IN 2023
ACCOUNTANCY
FINANCE
LOGISTICS
MARKETING
MEDIA
RETAIL
TECHNOLOGY

NUMBER OF VACANCIES
150-200 graduate jobs

LOCATIONS OF VACANCIES

STARTING SALARY FOR 2023
£25,000-£40,000

WORK EXPERIENCE
DEGREE
PLACEMENTS

UNIVERSITY PROMOTIONS DURING 2022-2023
BATH, BIRMINGHAM, BRISTOL, CAMBRIDGE, DURHAM, EDINBURGH, EXETER, GLASGOW, IMPERIAL COLLEGE LONDON, KING'S COLLEGE LONDON, LANCASTER, LEEDS, LIVERPOOL, LONDON SCHOOL OF ECONOMICS, LOUGHBOROUGH, MANCHESTER, NEWCASTLE, NORTHUMBRIA, NOTTINGHAM, NOTTINGHAM TRENT, OXFORD, SHEFFIELD, SOUTHAMPTON, ST ANDREWS, UNIVERSITY COLLEGE LONDON, WARWICK, YORK

MINIMUM ENTRY REQUIREMENTS
Varies by function
Relevant degree required for some roles.

APPLICATION DEADLINE
Year-round recruitment
Early application is advised.

FURTHER INFORMATION
www.Top100GraduateEmployers.com
Register now for the latest news, local promotions, work experience and graduate vacancies at THG.

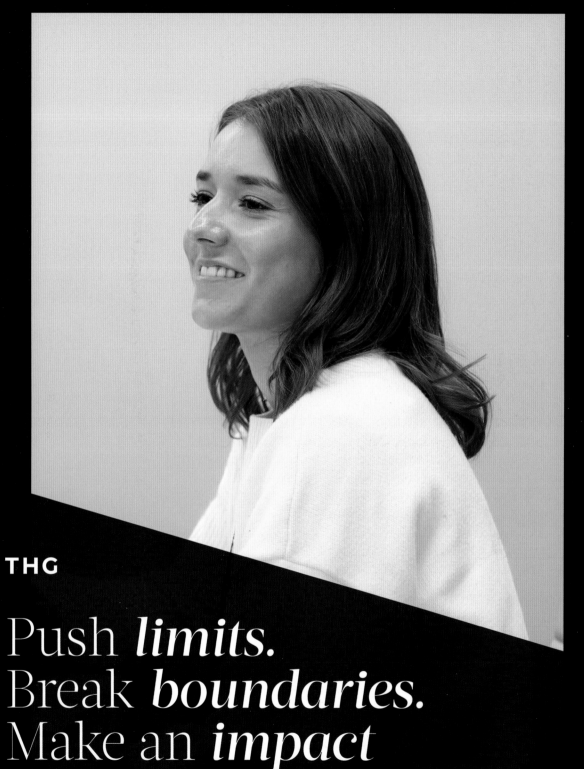

THG

Push *limits.*
Break *boundaries.*
Make an *impact*

Go further, *faster.*

Find out more about our exciting career paths at:
THG.com/careers

thinkahead.org

ThinkAheadOrg [f] recruitment@thinkahead.org [✉]
@ThinkAheadMH [𝕏] linkedin.com/company/think-ahead-org [in]
@ThinkAheadMH [◯] youtube.com/ThinkAheadMH [▶]

The Think Ahead programme is an innovative route into social work, for graduates and career-changers remarkable enough to make a real difference to people with mental health problems. The paid, two-year programme combines on-the-job learning, a master's degree and leadership training.

When someone is experiencing mental health problems, they need support in all aspects of their life. The things that matter most to them: housing, family, employment, community activities. Mental health social workers empower people to improve those social factors, helping them to flourish.

Specialising in adult mental health, Think Ahead trainees support people with severe and long-lasting mental health illnesses such as bipolar disorder, schizophrenia and personality disorders. Joining multidisciplinary teams in NHS Trusts or Local Authorities, they may work in a range of settings – such as Community Mental Health Teams, Older Adult Teams, Forensic Teams – alongside nurses, support workers, occupational therapists, psychologists and psychiatrists. The training programme begins with an intensive five-week course over the summer, preparing trainees for frontline work and equipping them with a grounding in mental health social work.

Trainees will then join a unit of four to six people. These units are across England and are in NHS Trusts or Local authorities. Each unit is led by a highly experienced Consultant Social Worker, and trainees share responsibility for the care of the people they work with. Trainees qualify as professional mental health social workers in the second year of the programme and are then able to work more independently. The programme culminates in a master's degree in social work. Leadership training also takes place, supporting trainees to become excellent social workers, and to work towards leading change in the future.

GRADUATE VACANCIES IN 2023
SOCIAL WORK

NUMBER OF VACANCIES
160 graduate jobs

LOCATIONS OF VACANCIES

STARTING SALARY FOR 2023
£17,200-£19,100
Tax-free training bursary for year 1. Starting salary dependant on location.

WORK EXPERIENCE
SUMMER INTERNSHIPS

UNIVERSITY PROMOTIONS DURING 2022-2023
ASTON, BATH, BIRMINGHAM, BRISTOL, CAMBRIDGE, CARDIFF, CITY, EAST ANGLIA, EDINBURGH, EXETER, IMPERIAL COLLEGE LONDON, KINGS COLLEGE LONDON, LEEDS, LIVERPOOL, LONDON SCHOOL OF ECONOMICS, LOUGHBOROUGH, MANCHESTER, NEWCASTLE, NOTTINGHAM, OXFORD, QUEEN MARY LONDON, SCHOOL OF AFRICAN STUDIES, SHEFFIELD, SOUTHAMPTON, SUSSEX, UNIVERSITY COLLEGE LONDON, WARWICK, YORK
Please check with your university careers service for full details of Think Ahead's local promotions and events.

MINIMUM ENTRY REQUIREMENTS
2.1 Degree

APPLICATION DEADLINE
Spring 2023
Early application is advised.

FURTHER INFORMATION
www.Top100GraduateEmployers.com
*Register now for the latest news, local promotions, work experience and graduate vacancies at **Think Ahead**.*

THINK

AHEAD

Think Ahead has given me a deeper understanding of the impact that mental illness can have on individuals.

Jan, Edinburgh graduate
and Think Ahead participant

thinkahead.org

TikTok

careers.tiktok.com

europe-campus@tiktok.com

As the leading destination for short-form mobile video, TikTok's mission is to inspire creativity and bring joy. With over 30,000 employees, TikTok has global offices in Los Angeles, New York, London, Paris, Berlin, Dubai, Mumbai, Singapore, Jakarta, Seoul, and Tokyo.

Always Day 1, Champion Diversity and Inclusion, Be Candid and Clear, Seek Truth and Be Pragmatic, Be Courageous and Aim for the Highest, and Grow Together, are the principles TikTok upholds to inspire creativity and spark joy. TikTok hires graduates from all degree disciplines, but the key behind its successes are those who can demonstrate a strong knowledge of the TikTok platform, as well as a passion for transforming the tech industry and innovating advertising.

Additionally, TikTok looks for candidates that can show that they have made an impact during their time at university through involvement in societies, clubs, organisations, and relevant internship and work experiences. TikTok seeks candidates who have a variety of strengths and passions to shape the diverse workforce and bring new perspectives. TikTok's flat structure provides employees with amazing opportunities to interact with senior business leaders early in their careers, taking on real responsibility and benefiting from the support and knowledge of their peers.

Whether it's selling an advertising solution to clients, driving the latest trends, hiring the next generation of talent at TikTok, or building an app that continues to disrupt the world of short-form mobile video, TikTok has full-time roles, graduate schemes, and internships available across teams such as sales, customer solutions, people operations, marketing, finance, legal, operations and engineering.

GRADUATE VACANCIES IN 2023
ENGINEERING
MARKETING
RESEARCH & DEVELOPMENT
SALES
TECHNOLOGY

NUMBER OF VACANCIES
No fixed quota

LOCATIONS OF VACANCIES

Vacancies also available in Europe and elsewhere in the world.

STARTING SALARY FOR 2023
£Competitive

WORK EXPERIENCE
DEGREE PLACEMENTS   SUMMER INTERNSHIPS

UNIVERSITY PROMOTIONS DURING 2022-2023
BATH, BIRMINGHAM, BRISTOL, CAMBRIDGE, CITY, DURHAM, EDINBURGH, ESSEX, IMPERIAL COLLEGE LONDON, KING'S COLLEGE LONDON, LANCASTER, LEICESTER, LIVERPOOL, MANCHESTER, NOTTINGHAM, OXFORD, SOUTHAMPTON, ST ANDREWS, UNIVERSITY COLLEGE LONDON, WARWICK, YORK
Please check with your university careers service for full details of TikTok's local promotions and events.

MINIMUM ENTRY REQUIREMENTS
Varies by function
Relevant degree required for some roles.

APPLICATION DEADLINE
31st December 2022

FURTHER INFORMATION
www.Top100GraduateEmployers.com
Register now for the latest news, local promotions, work experience and graduate vacancies at TikTok.

make impact happen

TikTok is the leading destination for short-form mobile video. Our mission is to inspire creativity and bring joy.

create to inspire

limitless possibilities

When you're borderless in your thinking, the opportunities are limitless at TikTok. There's no shortage of opportunities to build, innovate and lead.

Make impact happen with a career at TikTok.

🔍 careers.tiktok.com

TPP is a global digital health company. With more than 7,600 organisations using their solutions to care for over 50 million patients, their software is used across all health and social care settings, including GPs, emergency departments, hospitals, and mental health services.

TPP are committed to helping tackle global health challenges and delivering the future of healthcare. Their technology helps improve people's lives across the world, whether it is scheduling immunisations for millions of children, allowing doctors to manage care for elderly patients, helping governments with the prevention of outbreaks, or developing new machine learning algorithms for the early diagnosis of disease.

TPP's cloud database is one of the largest in the world, processing a billion transactions daily – more than the London Stock Exchange and Visa combined. In both 2017 and 2018, TPP were awarded the "Top Company for Graduates to Work For" by TheJobCrowd, and in 2021 they were named the "Top IT Development and Consulting" company to work for.

What makes TPP different from most graduate employers is that they want their new starters to feel empowered to voice their ideas from day one. There is no 'typical' TPP personality – they value a wide range of interests and backgrounds as essential to creating a diverse and talented team who can solve real-world problems every day. Ideally located in the hustle and bustle of Leeds, TPP is a great place for graduates to learn and begin their career in one of the UK's largest and fastest growing cities. With a plethora of cultural hotspots, restaurants, and bars of every kind, and striking countryside just a train ride away, Leeds has plenty to offer for everyone. The company provides excellent starting salaries, fantastic benefits, and outstanding annual pay reviews.

GRADUATE VACANCIES IN 2023

MARKETING
SALES
TECHNOLOGY

NUMBER OF VACANCIES
50+ graduate jobs

LOCATIONS OF VACANCIES

STARTING SALARY FOR 2023
£35,000-£50,000

WORK EXPERIENCE
SUMMER
INTERNSHIPS

UNIVERSITY PROMOTIONS DURING 2022-2023
BATH, BIRMINGHAM, BRADFORD, BRISTOL, CAMBRIDGE, DURHAM, EDINBURGH, IMPERIAL COLLEGE LONDON, KING'S COLLEGE LONDON, LANCASTER, LEEDS, LIVERPOOL, LONDON SCHOOL OF ECONOMICS, MANCHESTER, NEWCASTLE, NOTTINGHAM, OXFORD, QUEEN MARY LONDON, ROYAL HOLLOWAY, SHEFFIELD, SOUTHAMPTON, ST ANDREWS, UNIVERSITY COLLEGE LONDON, WARWICK, YORK
Please check with your university careers service for full details of TPP's local promotions and events.

MINIMUM ENTRY REQUIREMENTS
Varies by function
Relevant degree required for some roles.

APPLICATION DEADLINE
Year-round recruitment

FURTHER INFORMATION
www.Top100GraduateEmployers.com
Register now for the latest news, local promotions, work experience and graduate vacancies at TPP.

SOLVE PROBLEMS.
SAVE LIVES.

Software
Developer: **£50k**

Business
Analyst: **£50k**

Technical
Engineer: **£50k**

Service
Analyst: **£35k**

Account
Manager: **£50k**

Implementation
Specialist: **£35k**

NO EXPERIENCE REQUIRED

www.tpp-careers.com

f TPP Careers   🐦 @TPPCareers

📷 @tpp_careers   in TPP

careers.unilever.com/uk-graduates

Unilever is one of the world's largest consumer goods companies who make over 400 of the world's best loved brands. Unilever products help people look good, feel good, and get more out of life. With over 3.4 billion consumers using their products every day, their purpose is to make sustainable living commonplace.

Unilever have long held the belief that being a responsible, sustainable business drives superior performance. This has been integral to their values since their founder William Lever launched Sunlight Soap in the 1800's with the purpose to make cleanliness commonplace. Now a leading global organisation, they continually prove that brands with purpose grow and companies with purpose last. Committed to building an inclusive culture, they empower all employees to bring their authentic self to work.

To create the world's best loved brands, they understand the importance of building teams that reflect the diversity of the world we live in. Graduates are encouraged to get involved in Unilever's inclusive employee networks, for example, racial, LGBTQIA+, gender equality, disability, and carers networks. Many of which are led by graduates. Opportunities are available in HR, finance, supply chain, research and development, sales, marketing and technology and data management. Graduates on the Future Leaders Programme have a significant impact on the business and are given real responsibility from day one, preparing them to become a leader.

Unilever provide all graduates with continuous one-to-one business mentoring and support to assist their development and achievement of future goals. Unilever also supports graduates in achieving Chartered status and professional qualifications. Apply to Unilever for the opportunity to create a better world, a better business and a better you.

GRADUATE VACANCIES IN 2023

ENGINEERING
FINANCE
HUMAN RESOURCES
LOGISTICS
MARKETING
RESEARCH & DEVELOPMENT
SALES
TECHNOLOGY

NUMBER OF VACANCIES
50+ graduate jobs

LOCATIONS OF VACANCIES

STARTING SALARY FOR 2023
£32,000
Plus a £5,000 interest-free loan, an annual bonus and an annual salary increase.

WORK EXPERIENCE
DEGREE PLACEMENTS   SUMMER INTERNSHIPS

UNIVERSITY PROMOTIONS DURING 2022-2023
BATH, BIRMINGHAM, BRISTOL, CAMBRIDGE, CARDIFF, DURHAM, EDINBURGH, EXETER, GLASGOW, IMPERIAL COLLEGE LONDON, KING'S COLLEGE LONDON, LANCASTER, LEEDS, LIVERPOOL, LONDON SCHOOL OF ECONOMICS, LOUGHBOROUGH, MANCHESTER, NEWCASTLE, NOTTINGHAM, OXFORD, QUEEN MARY LONDON, SHEFFIELD, ST ANDREWS, UNIVERSITY COLLEGE LONDON, WARWICK
Please check with your university careers service for full details of Unilever's local promotions and events.

MINIMUM ENTRY REQUIREMENTS
Varies by function
Relevant degree required for some roles.

APPLICATION DEADLINE
Autumn 2022

FURTHER INFORMATION
www.Top100GraduateEmployers.com
Register now for the latest news, local promotions, work experience and graduate vacancies at Unilever.

CHANGE LED BY YOU

 Unilever has over 400 loved brands

 3.4 billion people use Unilever products everyday

 Unilever are the 2nd largest advertiser globally

 Available in over 190 countries

 2021 saw a turnover of €52 billion

 With over 148,000 purpose-led employees

Join now and make a real impact by helping us use this scale for good.
Unilever.com/careers/graduate

BETTER BUSINESS. A BETTER WORLD. A BETTER YOU.

Unlocked

unlockedgrads.org.uk

UnlockedGrads hello@unlockedgrads.org.uk

@UnlockedGrads 🐦 linkedin.com/school/unlocked-graduates 🔗

@UnlockedGrads 📷 youtube.com/unlockedgraduates ▶

Unlocked Graduates is a unique two-year leadership development programme that puts brilliant graduates at the heart of prison reform. Nearly half of all adult prisoners reoffend within one year of leaving prison, creating more victims, untold damage, and a cost of over £18 billion.

The problems facing prisons are some of the most complex in society. That's the challenge at the heart of the Unlocked Graduates two-year leadership development programme. Unlocked looks for ambitious graduates who are passionate about shaping the system for the better – as well as gaining a fully funded bespoke Master's degree, a highly competitive salary, the mentorship of an experienced prison officer, unique experiences, and development opportunities with key employers.

Combining academic study with real-world experience, Unlocked provides the platform to trial and assess solutions within prisons. And, in their second year, graduates get to write and present a policy paper to the Ministry of Justice.

As a prison officer, no two days are the same. Helping some of the most vulnerable and challenging people in society means being prepared for new situations – and being an advocate, negotiator, diplomat, and leader. It calls for a calm head, confidence, and problem-solving skills – all of which graduates develop with Unlocked. With real responsibility from day one, it's the rare chance to learn how to expertly face challenges head-on and hone expertise in leadership and communication – whether on the prison landing or in the Governor's office.

Many graduates choose to stay within the justice system after the programme, but no matter where their career takes them, Unlocked supports a growing network of change-makers. Being a prison officer is about so much more than locking up. With Unlocked Graduates, it can really open doors.

GRADUATE VACANCIES IN 2023
PRISON OFFICER

NUMBER OF VACANCIES
130 graduate jobs

LOCATIONS OF VACANCIES

STARTING SALARY FOR 2023
£23,000-£31,000

WORK EXPERIENCE
SUMMER INTERNSHIPS

UNIVERSITY PROMOTIONS DURING 2022-2023
ASTON, BATH, BIRMINGHAM, BRISTOL, BRUNEL, CAMBRIDGE, CARDIFF, DURHAM, EDINBURGH, ESSEX, EXETER, GLASGOW, IMPERIAL COLLEGE LONDON, KING'S COLLEGE LONDON, KENT, LANCASTER, LEEDS, LEICESTER, LIVERPOOL, LONDON SCHOOL OF ECONOMICS, LOUGHBOROUGH, MANCHESTER, NEWCASTLE, NOTTINGHAM, OXFORD, QUEEN MARY LONDON, ROYAL HOLLOWAY, SHEFFIELD, SOUTHAMPTON, SUSSEX, UEA, UNIVERSITY COLLEGE LONDON, WARWICK, YORK
Please check with your university careers service for full details of Unlocked's local promotions and events.

MINIMUM ENTRY REQUIREMENTS
2.1 Degree

APPLICATION DEADLINE
December 2022 - January 2023

FURTHER INFORMATION
www.Top100GraduateEmployers.com
Register now for the latest news, local promotions, work experience and graduate vacancies at Unlocked.

" **The nature of a prison can be very hectic with a lot of different situations that you have to deal with each day. I genuinely think that my time at Unlocked has prepared me for anything the corporate world will throw at me.**

Following my two years on the programme, I now work for a consultancy. I believe that my time working as a prison officer in the Unlocked Graduates programme really prepared me for this role because I was able to develop a lot of transferable skills, such as building relationships, always seeing the bigger picture, and making effective decisions under pressure.

Unlocked

unlockedgrads.org.uk

vodafone

From drones that deliver medicine to rural communities to bridging the digital divide for over a billion school kids globally and powering its European network with 100% renewable resources – Vodafone is a global tech communications leader that builds an inclusive, sustainable & digital future for all.

Vodafone's purpose is to build a digital society that enhances socio-economic progress, embraces everyone, and does not come at the cost of the planet. They are known for their technology – the connectivity they provide to 300 million+ customers and thousands of communities globally, continues to be critical in transforming lives and businesses.

They are restless and passionate about creating a better future, with the belief that when working together, humanity and technology can find answers and break new ground to achieve great feats. IoT that fights malnutrition, apps that connect the unbanked to financial services and a network that will help 1.6 billion people with rural connectivity from the edge of space – this and lots more to get involved in as part of their Graduate & Student programmes!

At Vodafone, graduates are inspired to experiment, try new things, and make mistakes. After all, it's the fastest way to learn. Their Discover Graduate programme allows talented young minds to gain hands-on experience, technical skills, personal and professional growth, and the opportunity to learn from industry experts – all at a company that's an industry game changer and in an environment which is diverse, inclusive and nurturing.

Graduates can make an impact in areas including Tech, Finance, Business, Commercial, and HR. Vodafone relies on innovators, collaborators, those who are open-minded and aren't afraid to push boundaries. A career with Vodafone is the chance to make the kind of impact you've always wanted to.

GRADUATE VACANCIES IN 2023

ENGINEERING

FINANCE

GENERAL MANAGEMENT

HUMAN RESOURCES

SALES

TECHNOLOGY

NUMBER OF VACANCIES
150-200 graduate jobs

LOCATIONS OF VACANCIES

STARTING SALARY FOR 2023
£30,000-£33,000
Plus an annual bonus.

WORK EXPERIENCE

DEGREE PLACEMENTS	SUMMER INTERNSHIPS

UNIVERSITY PROMOTIONS DURING 2022-2023
ASTON, BATH, BIRMINGHAM, BRUNEL, KING'S COLLEGE LONDON, LEEDS, LEICESTER, LOUGHBOROUGH, MANCHESTER, NOTTINGHAM, QUEEN MARY LONDON, READING, SOUTHAMPTON, SURREY, UNIVERSITY COLLEGE LONDON, WARWICK
Please check with your university careers service for full details of Vodafone's local promotions and events.

MINIMUM ENTRY REQUIREMENTS
2.2 Degree

APPLICATION DEADLINE
Varies by function

FURTHER INFORMATION
www.Top100GraduateEmployers.com
Register now for the latest news, local promotions, work experience and graduate vacancies at Vodafone.

Now you can turn hearts into actions.

Discover our Graduate Careers

So you're ready to turn your words into actions and ambitions into impact? Here's where it begins.

careers.vodafone.co.uk/graduate-programme

Together we can

WhiteCase   londontrainee@whitecase.com

@WhiteCase linkedin.com/company/white-&-case

@WhiteCase youtube.com/WhiteCaseGlobal

WHITE & CASE

White & Case is a global law firm of more than 2,500 lawyers worldwide. They've built an unrivalled network of 45 offices in 31 countries. That investment is the foundation for their client work in over 200 countries today. Many White & Case clients are multinational organisations with complex needs that require the involvement of multiple offices.

White & Case trainees will work on fast-paced, cutting-edge cross-border projects from the outset of their career. White & Case is looking to recruit ambitious trainees who have a desire to gain hands-on practical experience from day one and a willingness to take charge of their own career. They value globally minded citizens of the world who are eager to work across borders and cultures, and who are intrigued by solving problems within multiple legal systems.

The training contract consists of four six-month seats, one of which is guaranteed to be spent in one of their overseas offices.

They offer vacation scheme placements over the winter, spring, and summer, open days, and two-day insight schemes. These provide a great way to experience first-hand what life is like as a White & Case trainee as well as gain useful insight into the firm and the training they offer.

The firm's virtual learning programme offers the opportunity to gain first-hand insight into life as a White & Case trainee and experience the realities of cross-border law. There is no cost to access the platform, it is self-paced to fit around users' schedules, and no application form or legal knowledge is required. Students will gain insight into the fast-paced, cutting-edge projects their lawyers and trainees work on, and gain valuable skills by undertaking true-to-life legal tasks. Participation in the learning platform will be recognised on their application forms.

GRADUATE VACANCIES IN 2023
LAW

NUMBER OF VACANCIES
50 graduate jobs
For training contracts starting in 2025.

LOCATIONS OF VACANCIES

STARTING SALARY FOR 2023
£52,000

WORK EXPERIENCE
INSIGHT COURSES | DEGREE PLACEMENTS | SUMMER INTERNSHIPS

UNIVERSITY PROMOTIONS DURING 2022-2023
Please check with your university careers service for full details of White & Case's local promotions and events.

MINIMUM ENTRY REQUIREMENTS
2.1 Degree

APPLICATION DEADLINE
Please see website for full details.

FURTHER INFORMATION
www.Top100GraduateEmployers.com
Register now for the latest news, local promotions, work experience and graduate vacancies at **White & Case.**

Together we make a mark

Graduate careers in law

As a trainee in our London office, you will have the opportunity to work on challenging cross-border client matters providing you with international experience and exposure from day one. Join us and make your mark.

whitecasetrainee.com

1

of the only law firms to offer a guaranteed overseas seat

75

vacation scheme places per year in London

£52k

year-one starting salary

45

offices across 31 countries

50

trainees recruited per year in London

£140k

salary on qualification

WHITE & CASE

Useful Information

EMPLOYER	GRADUATE RECRUITMENT WEBSITE	EMPLOYER	GRADUATE RECRUITMENT WEBSITE
AIRBUS	airbus.com/en/careers/graduates	L'ORÉAL	careers.loreal.com
ALDI	aldirecruitment.co.uk	LATHAM & WATKINS	lwcareers.com
AMAZON	amazon.jobs	LIDL	lidlgraduatecareers.co.uk
AON	aonearlycareers.co.uk	LINKLATERS	careers.linklaters.com
ARCADIS	careers.arcadis.com/early-careers	LLOYDS BANKING GROUP	lloydsbankinggrouptalent.com
ASTRAZENACA	careers.astrazeneca.com/early-talent	MARS	careersmars.com/students-graduates
BAE SYSTEMS	baesystems.com/graduates	MI5	mi5.gov.uk/careers
BAKER MCKENZIE	uk-graduates.bakermckenzie.com	MORGAN STANLEY	morganstanley.com/campus
BANK OF AMERICA	campus.bankofamerica.com	MOTT MACDONALD	mottmac.com/careers
BBC	bbc.co.uk/youmakethebbc	NATWEST GROUP	jobs.natwestgroup.com
BCG	careers.bcg.com/students	NEWTON	workatnewton.com
BDO	careers.bdo.co.uk	NGDP FOR LOCAL GOVERNMENT	local.gov.uk/ngdp
BLACKROCK	careers.blackrock.com/early-careers	NHS	graduates.nhs.uk
BLOOMBERG	careers.blackrock.com/early-careers	P&G	pgcareers.com/location-uk-and-ireland
BP	bp.com/grads/uk	PA CONSULTING	paconsulting.com/careers/earlycareers
BT	bt.com/careers/early-careers	PENGUIN RANDOM HOUSE	penguinrandomhousecareers.co.uk
CIVIL SERVICE	faststream.gov.uk	PEPSICO	daretodomoreeurope.pepsico.com
CLYDE & CO	clydecoearlycareers.com	POLICE NOW	policenow.org.uk
CMS	cmsearlytalent.com	PWC	pwc.co.uk/careers
CREDIT SUISSE	credit-suisse.com/careers/en/students.html	REED SMITH	reedsmith.com/careers/regions/uk-graduates
DELOITTE	deloitte.co.uk/careers	ROLLS-ROYCE	careers.rolls-royce.com
DEUTSCHE BANK	careers.db.com/students-graduates	ROYAL NAVY	royalnavy.mod.uk/careers
DYSON	careers.dyson.com/early-careers	SANTANDER	santander.com/en/careers
ENTERPRISE	careers.enterprise.co.uk	SAVILLS	savills.co.uk/graduates
EVERSHEDS SUTHERLAND	eversheds-sutherland.com	SHELL	shell.co.uk/graduates
EY	ey.com/uk/students	SKY	careers.sky.com/earlycareers
FRESHFIELDS	freshfields.com/ukgraduates	SLAUGHTER AND MAY	slaughterandmay.com
FRONTLINE	thefrontline.org.uk/frontline-programme	SPECSAVERS	join.specsavers.com/uk
GCHQ	gchq-careers.co.uk	TEACH FIRST	teachfirst.org.uk/training-programme
GOLDMAN SACHS	gs.com/careers/students	THG	thg.com
GOOGLE	google.com/students	THINK AHEAD	thinkahead.org
GRANT THORNTON	trainees.grantthornton.co.uk	TIKTOK	careers.tiktok.com
GSK	gsk.com/en-gb/careers	TPP	tpp-careers.com
HALEON	haleon.com/careers/early-talent	UNILEVER	careers.unilever.com/uk-graduates
HSBC	hsbc.com/earlycareers	UNLOCKED	unlockedgrads.org.uk
J.P MORGAN	jpmorgan.com/careers	VODAFONE	careers.vodafone.co.uk/graduate-programme
KPMG	kpmgcareers.co.uk	WHITE & CASE	whitecasetrainee.com
KUBRICK	kubrickgroup.com/join-us		